Get Carter and Beyond:
THE CINEMA OF MIKE HODGES

Get Carter and Beyond:
THE CINEMA OF
MIKE HODGES

Steven Paul Davies

Batsford

A catalogue record for this book is available from
the British Library.

ISBN 0 7134 8790 9

Printed in Spain

Designed by Zeta Jones

Volume © B T Batsford 2002

First published in 2002 by
B T Batsford
9 Blenheim Court, Brewery Road
London N7 9NT

A member of **Chrysalis** Books plc

CONTENTS

ACKNOWLEDGEMENTS

The major part of this book comprises interviews recorded with Mike Hodges over the last two years, most conducted at his home in Dorset. Principle thanks, therefore, go to Mike for his willingness and ability to respond incisively and honestly to my continued questioning! His co-operation also extended to providing the numerous behind-the scenes stills that appear throughout the book.

Many thanks also to Clive Owen, George Segal, Michael Caine, John Glen, Alex Cox, Wolfgang Suschitsky, Andrew Pulver at *The Guardian* and to Paul Mayersberg for his kind interest and support.

Picture Acknowledgements
Get Carter illustrations courtesy of Wolfgang Suschitzky; *Dandelion Dead* illustrations courtesy of Granada; *Croupier* illustrations courtesy of Simon Mein/FilmFour. All production stills courtesy of Mike Hodges.

FOREWORD

More than any other form of art, except possibly architecture, film-making, the film-maker's life work, is about what might have been.

With different actors, or with more money, or at a different time, or with a different promotional campaign, we might have been looking at something other than what we see. This is not what most audiences speculate on, although occasionally critics do, but it is a large preoccupation for the film-maker, before, during and after the making of a film. Steven Paul Davies' book on and with Mike Hodges is almost as much about what didn't happen as what did. It could have adopted as a subtitle the title of his 1983 TV film, *Missing Pieces*.

Few film-makers today are inclined to admit to discontinuity in their work. It would hint at confusion and failure. Samuel Beckett's axiom "Fail again. Fail better," is not the ideal motto for contemporary celebrity-success. But uncertainty is ever the sleeping partner of ambition.

The narrative here is resolutely chronological. It cannot and will not paper over the life cracks or plane out the art warps. Oddly, the effect of reading the whole book is like hearing a journal of the frustrations and elevations that alternate in the making of a *single* film. Mike's voice-over throughout makes everything untidily life-like rather than formally art-like. It's more of a character piece than a plot.

It poses the interesting question of how far a man's long-time work reflects his personality and behaviour, especially in such a social form as film where he is not alone. In a glasshouse society where friendship is illusory and agendas are hidden there will inevitably be a preponderance of villains over heroes. Film-life is a devious affair and engenders personal prejudice as a defence. But then what are our prejudices if not the illegitimate children of our convictions?

Mike's best films, *The Terminal Man* and *Black Rainbow*, both commercial failures, are about manipulation. But they are not, as films, manipulative. None of their characters invites easy identification. Thank God. They are decidedly *other* people. An only child myself, I recognise in Mike a similar unsentimental sensibility.

A couple of detached sibling-free voyeurs observing what the world does to its unfortunate inhabitants. People like us. A world as Le Corbusier observed, about the nature and purpose of a house, is "a machine for living in".

It's unlikely that this book would have been published without the recent success of *Croupier*. From being written off, Mike is now being written up. And at the age of three score years and ten. Ainsi va le monde. The number 70 reminds me of an occasion when Mike and I were lunching with a sympathetic critic who described *Croupier* as somehow coming from the Seventies, in which decade he thought it might have fared better. This was a year or more before the US release. It was therefore an unexpected delight that American audiences were completely unaware they were applauding a 30-year-old movie as if it were new: what might not have been, as it were.

PAUL MAYERSBERG

Cannes, June 2002

"It's all numbers," the croupier thought. "The spin of the wheel. The turn of the card. The time of your life. Date of your birth. Year of your death. In the 'Book of Numbers', the Lord said, 'Thou shalt count thy steps'."
Jack Manfred in *Croupier* (1998)

Introduction

I FIRST BUMPED into Mike Hodges in January 1998, at the Institute of Contemporary Art in London, for the launch of an earlier book of mine, *Alex Cox: Film Anarchist*. At the time, although I didn't realize it, he was in the middle of putting together *Croupier*. A few months after our initial meeting, I saw *Croupier* at a preview screening in London.

In the warm, dark recess of that movie auditorium in Soho I watched struggling writer Jack Manfred (Clive Owen) take a job as a croupier to make ends meet, and then dispassionately observe the losers at his table. Eighty-seven minutes later, life was a different prospect altogether. Hodges, with a highly intelligent script by Paul Mayersberg, had highlighted my own personal chaos. As the credits rolled, I picked up my diary, my filofax and my mobile phone. But by this point, I could at least hear my own personal wheel spinning.

Croupier, I thought, was a fantastic piece of filmmaking and I knew I had to meet with Mike again. Thanks to an introduction from Alex Cox, we met at a crowded pub in North London, and it was there that he agreed to help with this biography.

Hodges' career has been marked with enormous critical and varying commercial success. Features as disparate as *Get Carter* (1971), *Flash Gordon* (1980), *Black Rainbow* (1989) and *Croupier* (1998) are some of the seminal films in their respective genres.

In fact, Hodges' versatility seems nearly endless. *Get Carter* (1971), was his debut feature film. A seminal thriller that redefined the gangster genre for British moviemakers, it firmly established him as a master filmmaker. But even after this initial mainstream success, Hodges wasn't interested in submitting to the kinds of formulas that might ensure great box office. Consider, for instance, his next two films: *Pulp* (1972), an off-beat satirical comedy, quietly subversive in its approach; and *The Terminal Man* (1974), a dark and disturbing science-fiction picture, highly effective in driving home a serious warning to society. Admittedly, Hodges *was* attracted to one mega-budget project, signing up to direct the dazzling, special-effects-filled *Flash Gordon* (1980) for Dino de Laurentiis, arguably the most successful screen adaptation of a fantasy comic strip, which achieved an international gross of over $100 million.

Squaring the Circle (1984), his innovative television film about an

Previous page:

Clive Owen as Jack Manfred in Mike Hodges'

Croupier (1998)

imaginary confrontation between the Solidarity movement, the Church and the Communist party received the International Emmy as the year's best production. And in *Black Rainbow* (1989), Hodges riveted audiences with a multi-layered supernatural thriller that gave Rosanna Arquette the best role of her career as a medium who begins predicting the truth.

This book looks at the whole of Hodges' career, and so also details the disappointments along the way. Despite delivering most of his films exactly how he'd wanted them, Hodges has suffered from the vagaries of distribution, especially in the UK. *The Terminal Man* (1974), was not distributed here at all and *Black Rainbow* (1989), although critically acclaimed, was given a token UK release because the distributor was going bust. Of course, what happens to Hodges' films after they've been finished is out of his control.

Major edits were made to *A Prayer for the Dying* (1987) behind Hodges' back, forcing him to disown the films and *Florida Straits*, made a year earlier, was also tampered with.

However, re-editing by producers is common, so perhaps Hodges should count himself lucky it has only happened to him on these two occasions. The film industry is a brutal business and there are certainly far easier ways to earn a living. Thankfully, most of Hodges' films have survived creatively intact. "I, and my films, might have been lost in the shuffle of film fashion," he says, "if my number hadn't come up with *Croupier* – but it did." To me, the brilliance of *Croupier* wasn't a huge surprise. Before seeing it, I'd obviously already watched and loved *Get Carter* but was particularly fond of his lesser-known sci-fi thriller *The Terminal Man* and the little-seen *Black Rainbow*. What *did* surprise me was hearing that *Croupier* had been disowned by those who had commissioned it.

Fortunately, the film became a sleeper success in the US. After it spent over a year gathering dust on the shelves on Channel Four, *Croupier* was taken on by a New York distribution company called The Shooting Gallery and screened in 17 cities across the States. Critics, starved for intellectual content, acclaimed Hodges as "a master of the medium" (Andrew Sarris, *New York Observer*). It was named on over 75 US national lists as one of 2000's Ten Best Films, including: *Time Out*

New York, *The Los Angeles Times* and *The Washington Post*. New York's prestigious Museum of Modern Art even held a Hodges Retrospective in January 2001. By this time, *Croupier* was already booked in at more than 100 screens across America.

Following the picture's successful run in the US, where it grossed over $8 million at the box office, FilmFour re-released *Croupier* in the UK. Yet more great reviews followed and suddenly Hodges was hip again.

Two years ago, when FilmFour decided not to distribute *Croupier,* Hodges seriously contemplated retiring from filmmaking. Why bother when he could happily spend his time to painting, writing and gardening at his home in Dorset? Thankfully, *Croupier*'s unexpected success has given Hodges a new lease of creative life. First came a documentary about serial-killer films for the Independent Film Channel in America, for which he talked to the likes of David Fincher, Michael Mann, Richard Fleischer and John McNaughton. His play, a surreal comedy about the movie business called *Shooting Stars and Other Heavenly Pursuits*, opened in London during the summer of 2001 and Hodges will complete 2002 by delivering his new feature, *I'll Sleep When I'm Dead*, which reunites him with *Croupier* star Clive Owen.

Over the years, a few critics have complained that Hodges' films lack the kind of thematic unity that film scholars treasure so highly. True, he loves new challenges and creating new worlds and, on the surface, none of these pictures seem to resemble any of the others. But look again. His immaculately crafted films reflect the kaleidoscopic nature of modern life, inverting cinematic convention as they unfold. Most of them are rooted in a recognizable contemporary world. A world full of corruption and uncertainty. Commonality also lies in the solid, creative professionalism of their construction and in the passionate direction evident throughout.

Hodges continues to garner respect from movie-goers and critics alike for creating some of the most original movies of the last 30 years. This fully authorized biography provides a comprehensive examination of all of Hodges' films and television projects. It also unveils his opinions on the British film industry, including the recent spate of Carteresque gangster flicks, and re-tells the fairytale story of how the roulette wheel finally found Mike Hodges' number ...

Steven Paul Davies

The Early Years

"You have to make a choice in life. Be a gambler or a croupier. Then live with your decision come what may."
Jack Manfred in Croupier

Mike Hodges was born on 29 July 1932, in Bristol where his father worked as a commercial sales representative for a tobacco company. While Hodges' father was Church of England, his mother was a Roman Catholic and, as in all such "mixed marriages" of the 1930s and 1940s, the Catholic parent of the family made sure the child was also educated as a Catholic. Hodges' mother, however, didn't like the local convent and so in 1939, a 7-year-old Hodges was sent from Bristol to Prior Park College, a boarding school in Bath run by the Irish Christian Brothers.

The influential Irish Roman Catholic religious Order, involved in teaching generations of youngsters around the world, was later disbanded for harbouring pederasts. They even issued an unprecedented high-profile public apology for sexual and other abuse inflicted over years in its institutions. Recently, the congregation of the Christian Brothers in Ireland took out half-page advertisements in Irish newspapers admitting that some victims' complaints had been ignored. The admission followed a number of prosecutions initiated against members of the Order, over sex and other crimes, often dating back decades.

Inquiries into abuse by Roman Catholic clerics of school and orphanage pupils developed into a huge probe of allegations dating back to the 1930s and involving hundreds of people over decades. Over 50 former and serving members of the brutalized and supposedly celibate Order are being investigated for complaints against them of sexual and physical abuse of the young persons in their care, and the enquiry into the running of schools by the Christian Brothers has mushroomed into a general investigation of abuse involving children in state-funded, religious-run schools and orphanages.

Hodges describes his own time spent at the Irish Christian Brothers-run college as "grim". There until he was 15, he simply learned to survive:

"They used the strap and the cane and for serious offences the punishment was a ritualized affair, like an execution. We used to sleep in small cubicles and the punishment was enacted straight after lights out. The victim was taken from his cubicle to the communal washroom which was at centre of the dormitory, bent over a stool

Previous page: A young Mike Hodges, during his years in the Navy

and thrashed. Everyone else could hear the swish of the cane and the screams and grunts of the child. In retrospect it probably seems more callous than it was. At the time you just accepted it. We were boarders and there was literally no one you could turn to.

"During my time at the junior school, St Peter's, there was a house master who would come to the cubicles after dark and touch us sexually. It wasn't buggery, not even masturbation. He just seemed to want to touch young flesh. He was a very sad character. However, during the summer holidays my mother overheard me talking with a school friend about how I'd pretend to be asleep when he came to the cubicle, as it seemed to put him off. Our mothers, being good Catholics, were shocked. They went to the headmaster, but of course the house master denied it all. Amazingly, we were then sent back. Can you imagine that happening now? People were so innocent then. It was during the war and they believed everything they were told. I was only 10 or 11 but I already knew differently.

"That house master never spoke to me again, which was a relief. Until then he must have liked me. He even made me librarian. I wasn't a voracious reader but I did love books and words and I remember coming across the word 'rape' and asking him what it meant. He immediately dodged the question and said it was something you used in the garden!

"School was a painful period of my life, a period of survival. But of course it was during the war and so the whole country was trying to survive."

One significant part of Hodges' school life was the fortnightly film screening, every other Sunday night. This was his introduction to cinema with the musical comedy *Top Hat* (1935), starring Ginger Rogers and Fred Astaire, being the first film Hodges ever saw. The films were carefully chosen, including Spencer Tracy fighting the Indians in *Northwest Passage* (1939), as well as other war movies and historical adventures.

On leaving school at 15, Hodges returned to the family home in Salisbury, Wiltshire, and soon realized he wanted to work in the cinema, a result of his teenage years spent in the local movie houses in the "dark rooms of escape". There were three cinemas in the town

– the Odeon, the Regal and the ABC – and because his parents didn't really approve of him using all of his spare time watching movies, Hodges found himself having to lie a lot in order to visit all three venues, not to mention the Sunday films.

Hodges soon became a big fan of Billy Wilder as well as the work of the writer-director team of Michael Powell and Emeric Pressburger, in addition to B-movie classics such as 1955's *Kiss Me Deadly*. He was particularly intrigued by Wilder's scathing view of early Hollywood in *Sunset Boulevard* (1950) and entranced by Powell and Pressburger's Technicolor films, from the panoramic and witty *The Life and Death of Colonel Blimp* (1943) to the striking and strange *Gone to Earth* (1950). As a teenager Hodges was also captivated by Joseph Mankiewicz's jaundiced look at the showbiz battle zone of Broadway in *All About Eve* (1950).

Another director Hodges found fascinating was the Cypriot filmmaker Michael Cacoyannis:

"Cacoyannis was the first foreign director I fell in love with. I didn't know it at the time but he had a British cinematographer called Walter Lassally. *A Girl in Black* (1956) is an astonishing film. I'll never forget it. I went to see it at the Odeon in Salisbury. Because it was a foreign film, it ended up as the B-movie in a double bill. I have no idea how it ended up in Salisbury; nor did the audience, most of them were talking all through it. I remember standing up in the cinema and telling them to shut up. What a prig! I simply couldn't understand why these arseholes were talking through such an amazing film, one which was far better than any A-film I'd seen for years. There is an extraordinary scene in which the heroine, a widow, leaves the village to meet a young man. They are seen having sex, and by the time she returns the word is out. The torture of her walk back; everyone turns their back on her. She is disgraced, and alone, as good as dead. It is still, to this day, for me one of the most awful and horrifying scenes I've ever watched. How an audience could not react to that just seemed impossible and I got very angry."

It's not surprising that Hodges retreated to the cinema a lot, mainly to escape the mundane world of life as a trainee accountant. He had wanted to apply for the stage course at the Royal Academy

of Dramatic Arts (RADA) but his parents wouldn't hear of it. His father wanted him to have a profession. He was good at maths and it was decided he'd be a chartered accountant. A deal was struck and he passed his exams to become an accountant on the understanding he could do what he wanted afterwards.

Hodges qualified in 1955, but, while waiting to do his National Service, preferred working as a postman, farm labourer and bed salesman to a career in accountancy. At the age of 22 he was conscripted into the Royal Navy. From 1955 to 1957 he served in the Fishery Protection Squadron. As a Chartered Accountant he could have had an automatic commission but chose to serve, on the lower deck, on board HMS *Coquette* and later HMS *Wave*. He sailed to Iceland during the time of the cod wars, Norway, Sweden and

Holland, as well as docking in almost every fishing port around Britain. The experience gave him a whole new slant on life:

"It was probably the best thing that ever happened to me up until then and perhaps the best decision of my life. Being on the lower deck of a small ship, working on minesweepers, changed me for ever. It was my university. From a lower middle-class background I entered this world which I didn't know existed. I went in as a child of true blue parents, a private school, a profession, and a Young Conservative – came out a rabid Socialist. My politics were radically changed when I saw the places where people lived and the social deprivation of Hull, Grimsby, Lowestoft, all the ports. The conditions in which people lived was horrifying. Hogarthian. Seeing

The World in Action *team in 1964 with Hodges bottom left*

the underbelly of my country would later very much influence my approach to *Get Carter*."

After his Navy stint was over Hodges went to London. There he managed to get a job as an operator with Teleprompters Limited. "Great big yellow rolls like toilet paper, with the script typed in oversized letters, for TV presenters and performers to read from. It was all live in those days," he recalls. The company was owned by the renowned film producer, Harry Allan Towers. The job only paid £10 a week but got Hodges his opening in the television and film industry. Although "the cameramen hated you because the prompters added extra weight to their cameras", Hodges was in a position to observe what was happening in the studios at the BBC, the different ITV companies and even in the film studios. "Studios can be daunting places when you first go into them. Now I was able to observe all of the intricacies of film and television production and on my own terms. I was able to watch directors at work and quickly realized that a lot of them were complete chumps. I knew I could do better!"

On one trip up to Manchester for a production at ABC, Hodges found himself sitting on a train with Sidney Newman, the executive producer of ABC Television's *Armchair Theatre*. Overhearing Newman saying that he was looking for a drama based around the issue of euthanasia, Hodges quickly completed a play entitled *Some Will Cry Murder* and sent it in to the programme's production office. It never made it to the screen but led to other offers.

"I was privy to all the fallout in society ... but like a lot of young people I was still idealistic ... I still dreamt we were going to change the world."
Mike Hodges

Euston Films' Lloyd Shirley, then head of advertising magazines for ABC, asked Hodges to write for him. This meant a sudden leap from £10 a week to £25 a script so he abandoned his job as a teleprompter operator. Aside from advertising magazines, he wrote for *Once Upon a Time*, a children's series which starred such personalities as Spike

Milligan and Ron Moody; *Catching a Woman's Eye*, a documentary about designing and marketing women's products; and *Rave*, a light-entertainment feature starring Tony Tanner.

When Shirley became ABC's head of features, he made Hodges editor of *Sunday Break*, a religious programme for young people. It was policy to hire an atheist as editor to maintain a quizzical stance. That suited Hodges fine. A year later, after making an impression with an hilarious one-off documentary about funeral directors entitled *The British Way Of Death*, he landed his "dream job" as a producer/director on ITV's documentary series *World in Action*. "In its early day it was such a great programme," recalls Hodges. "The audience never knew the subject matter until it actually aired. It banked on their curiosity, and it worked. It's a lesson I took to. The style was a tabloid approach, but tabloids were different then, and the programmes were extraordinarily lively. By comparison the BBC's current affairs flagship, *Panorama*, was very plonky. These few years gave me time to accumulate knowledge of shooting, choosing lenses and watching more experienced directors at work."

However, it was also during his time spent on *World in Action* that Hodges honed his quizzical worldview. Jet-setting between global flash points and war zones, his encounters with young soldiers in Vietnam, far-right presidential candidates in Dallas and battered union organizers in Detroit fuelled his "total disillusionment with America" as the summer of love disintegrated. "The US administration and its citizens seemed divorced from each other. In a sense that has happened, only we didn't realize our dreams were to be harnessed to money, profit was to replace trust."

After two years on *World in Action*, Hodges moved from current affairs into the arts, taking the executive producer role, as well as that of director, on ITV's *Tempo*. The programme had been started under Ken Tynan's editorship, having a primetime slot and big budget. But the budget had shrunk to £2,000 per programme and the transmission time was now 2:15 on a Sunday afternoon. Even so Hodges was happy with the change in direction, having tired of current affairs: "I'd had a belly full. In current affairs you leap from one subject to another, from one interviewee to another, you can begin to feel like a leech, sucking what you want from people."

Hodges was neither frightened nor respectful of televised "culture", if anything he objected to these unnatural barriers. Refusing to cover the current fads, with *Tempo*, he tried a journalistic approach, always with a critical edge. Hodges was responsible for films on Harold Pinter, Orson Welles, Jaques Tati, Jean-Luc Godard, Lee Strasberg, Alain Robbe-Grillet and Charles Eames. Hodges came to believe there shouldn't be *any* arts series on television – or religious ones: "They form a kind of ghetto. And there's a desperation finding material to fill them. Indeed, towards the end of *Tempo* we tried to blow them away completely. Just look at *The South Bank Show*. It's dead on its feet. If not dead, tired. I can't watch it any

Orson Welles talks to Mike Hodges for the arts series Tempo

more. The programmes feel cheap and desperate now."

During his two years at the helm of *Tempo*, Hodges gathered around him a highly talented team of directors – Dick Fontaine, James Goddard and Denis Postle. So, at the end of 1966, they came up with *New Tempo*, a series of nine films all with generic titles: "We wanted to give the films a sense of freedom so that the film itself would be the art form. While the content was of prime importance we sought different ways of presenting it." The nine films produced were *The Information Explosion, Disposability, Heroes, Noise, Nostalgia, Stimulants, Leisure, Violence* and a final reprise which took elements from the previous eight. All were very experimental. The opener caused viewers to jam the switchboards at ABC with complaints. "There was so much time-lapse photography it gave people indigestion. Too close to Sunday lunch was my excuse," recalls Hodges. "More than 200 people phoned in because they either thought it was awful or too unsettling. Only one person thought it was fantastic." Hodges had wanted *New Tempo* to be the end of the

Hodges and a jovial Welles during a break in filming for Tempo

arts programme for ever but, instead, the series created an industry buzz. *New Society* ran a feature on it and the advertising agencies became great advocates, always helpful in commercial television. Having made such an impact, the programmes were repeated just six months later, unprecedented for ITV at the time. "Unfortunately it didn't change anything. It's fascinating how back then we really thought we could change things. How naïve we were. Nothing changes. Maybe history is cyclical – not progressive."

The following year, Hodges produced and directed the six-part children's serial *The Tyrant King* (1967) as a way of convincing ABC to switch drama on to film. "By now I was addicted to 16mm as a pliable, fast-moving medium in which to work. More importantly I wanted to convince them that they had better sales outlets compared with video. I realized that the economics of the venture was the key. With *The Tyrant King*, I proved that you could do good stuff on film for a reasonable price."

After proving his point, Hodges was commissioned to write two film scripts. He was also hired to produce and direct the 90-minute slots for Thames Television's *Playhouse* series. The first of these location-shot thrillers was *Suspect* (1968). This Chabrolesque murder story is a very slow-moving, low-key psychological thriller, set in a rural English village, which draws together the parallel stories of a police search for a murdered child and the breakdown of a middle-class couple's marriage – a subtle comparison between murder physical and murder psychological. A highly personal film, the script for *Suspect* is partly based on Hodges' own marriage, his parents' marriage and even features his late wife Jean (whom he'd married in 1963) and two young children, Ben and Jake. Hodges' earlier experience in documentaries is in evidence as he slowly charts the bleak police investigation into the 11-year-old girl's disappearance. Pieced out in odd little fragments, *Suspect* eventually builds into an unsettling, matter-of-fact portrait of a sexual predator on the loose in the English countryside. The film stars Rachel Kempson, Bryan Marshall and George Sewell.

The second film was the fast-moving *Rumour* (1969) which dealt with a journalist's foray into the underworld. (These two films were

to be the prototype for the formation of Thames subsidiary Euston
Films, which five years later was to launch *The Sweeney*). A much
more hard-edged piece in comparison with *Suspect*, it is the story of
a cynical tabloid newspaper gossip columnist who unwittingly
becomes a pawn in a particularly nasty political conspiracy. Hodges'
film looks at the freedom of the press and what happens when it
abuses that freedom. Michael Coles stars as the muckraking Fleet
Street hack who gets drawn into the murder of a young hooker with
supposed political connections. In the end, the scandal he's
investigated invokes dark forces that destroy him, and the story's
brilliant final twist is reminiscent of Nicolas Roeg's *Performance*.

Hodges celebrates his 39th birthday during the making of Get Carter *(1971)*

Filmed entirely on location in London, Hodges uses long lenses throughout, resulting in a sense of watching from a distance. This voyeuristic style would later become a trademark and continued with *Get Carter* (1971).

Another of Hodges' trademarks is his attention to detail and love for giving clues and warnings to what is about to happen to his characters. In *Rumour*, Coles, as the hero of the piece, is first seen driving a flashy pink Oldsmobile along the Westway in London. At the time, a cinema stood behind the flyover, its marquee peeping above the parapet. *Goodbye Columbus* was playing there. By carefully excluding the word *Columbus* from the shot, the hero is introduced with the word *Goodbye* in large letters behind him. In the end, he is killed by a hit man.

Hodges says the experimental style he adopted for *Rumour* was the result of his love for the films of Jean-Luc Godard:

"I love the sense of freedom which Godard brought to his films. He would digress or simply decide to just repeat a shot. It was totally intuitive. In truth, *Rumour* should be dedicated to him as there's no doubt that I felt that same sense of freedom. For example, during the shooting I was travelling back and forth through the Blackwall tunnel and I felt that as it was so strange and eerie I wanted to somehow use it in the film but I didn't know how. Anyway I had my cameraman attach the camera to the roof of my little Fiat and drove through the tunnel two or three times. When I then came to edit the film I realized the importance of my intuition. The shots gave me the start and end of my film as a descent into hell. I even quoted one of my favourite T S Elliot quotes: 'I think we are in rat's alley'. A script is only on paper yet for some it's like concrete. It should be a living, changing entity and if it isn't there is something deeply wrong with what you're doing."

An ambitious mix of 1940s' noir and late 1960s' psychedelia, *Rumour* incorporates a disturbing exploration of the themes of corruption, manipulation and the abuse of power, which Hodges would later expand in *Get Carter* (1971). It also paints a vivid picture of the London underworld he would revisit decades later in *Croupier* (1998) and *I'll Sleep When I'm Dead* (2002). *Rumour* also marks Hodges' first use of voice-over narration. These important themes and stylistic devices are prevalent in much of Hodges' subsequent work.

Despite causing a minor outcry from hacks in Fleet Street, *Rumour* was a big success and got nominated for the 1969 Prix D'Italia, the international award for the best dramatic show of the year. It also brought Hodges to the attention of the film producer, Michael Klinger, and led to the invitation to write and direct *Get Carter*...

Criminal Past: Get Carter

"In the beginning is the end – but we still go on."
Samuel Beckett

Early in 1970, Michael Klinger, the producer of Roman Polanski's first two British films, *Repulsion* and *Cul-de-Sac*, bought the film rights to Ted Lewis's then-unpublished novel *Jack's Return Home*, about a London racketeer who sets out to discover the cause of his brother's sudden death. "Immediately I could see there was a film there," recalled Klinger, who had realized he could exploit the recent upsurge of interest in the underworld aroused by the trial of the Richardson and Kray gangs. A close friend of Klinger's, Robert Littman, was Head of European Production for MGM and looking for new projects. When the two got together to discuss Lewis's novel, a deal was soon struck to make it into a hard-hitting, realistic gangster film.

Klinger had been thinking about Michael Caine in the role of Jack Carter, and the night after seeing Hodges' *Rumour* on television, he called Caine's agent, Dennis Selinger. The two men discussed both

"So calculatedly cool and soulless and nastily erotic that it seems to belong to a new era of virtuoso viciousness."
Pauline Kael on *Get Carter*

the novel and how impressed they were by Hodges' second TV film. When it was agreed that Hodges was to be approached to direct the adaptation of Lewis's book, Selinger called Caine. Having also seen *Rumour*, Caine signed up: "One of the other reasons I wanted to do it was because I had this image on screen of a Cockney ersatz Errol Flynn. The Cockney bit was all right but the ersatz suggested I'm artificial, and the Errol Flynn tag misses the point. One's appearance distracts people from one's acting. Carter was real," claims Caine.

Hodges had never adapted a novel to the screen before, and at first felt obliged to the author. He sent Lewis copies of the script as it evolved, making sure to keep the writer informed at every stage. "It was an extraordinary time for both of us," says Hodges. "We were both moving into another, bigger league. I subsequently heard that Ted had been desperate to write the script himself. He was a lovely

Previous page:
Michael Caine as
vicious London
gangster Jack
Carter

man and I had no idea at the time that he wanted to do it. That saddened me."

The first page of Ted Lewis's novel reads: "I was the only one in the compartment. My slip-ons were off. My feet were up. *Penthouse* was dead. I'd killed off the *Standard* twice. I had three nails left. Doncaster was forty minutes off."

However, Hodges' final script deviates straight away. While Caine's Carter is still an obsessional man, he pops pills and certainly doesn't bite his nails. He's also a man who points and doesn't say "please", unlike the Carter in Lewis's original novel.

Extract from Hodges' screenplay:

Int. the long bar. Night
A couple of youths are playing records on the juke box. An old man sits in the corner reading a newspaper.
Carter enters through the swing door and a weedy barman comes to serve him.
Carter: Pint of bitter.
The barman picks up a glass mug and begins to draw the beer. Carter snaps his fingers at him.
Carter: In a thin glass.
The barman sighs petulantly, transfers the beer into a thin glass and puts it on the counter.

Another deviation in Hodges' script is the location. Lewis came from Scunthorpe and had written it with his home town in mind. In fact, in the book, Carter changes trains at Doncaster and heads for a town with no name. All we know is that it's a steel town. The problem of where to set the film was solved when Hodges remembered his time in the National Service:

"On a minesweeper in the navy, I'd literally floated into every major fishing port in the British Isles. I told Klinger about the places I'd seen and off we trolled up the east coast in his Cadillac. Although the book wasn't set anywhere specific, the landscape was a major player in the piece. It was important that Jack Carter came from a hard, deprived background, a place he never wanted to go back to.

*Caine with co-star
Geraldine Moffat
(Glenda)*

There would have been no morality to this tale until you saw where he came from. When we got on the road I quickly realized that the east coast had changed radically since I'd been there in the early fifties. The only place that had survived the developers was Newcastle-upon-Tyne, but only just. We got there just in time. When I'd been in the navy I'd only been to North Shields, which was pretty grim, but this time I came by land which brought me to Newcastle. I fell in love with it as soon as I saw it. So that's where I set it. An important decision that! I stayed on after Klinger and the Cadillac had left for London and began to fit all the extraordinary locations I found into the script. This gives just a feeling for the place. There was a massive club there called *La Dolce Vita*. Can you imagine that – a club in Newcastle in the late sixties named after a Fellini film?"

It turned out that *La Dolce Vita* had been the scene of a real-life murder three years before Hodges made *Get Carter*, aspects of which he decided to work into his script:

"The body of Angus Sibbet had been found under a railway bridge close to the *La Dolce Vita*. He'd been shot. Two men, Dennis Stafford and Michael Luvaglio, were arrested and convicted. It was the motive for this killing that provided much background detail in the film, as well as an important location – Cyril Kinnear's home.

"Luvaglio was the youngest brother of Vincent Landa, a flamboyant entrepreneur who had lined his fruit machines with false bottoms, and then did a bunk with the swag to his villa in Majorca.

"Both Luvaglio and Angus Sibbet had been involved in extracting the money from the machines. Sibbet got greedy; end of story; end of Sibbet. It later transpired that a hit man, not unlike Carter, had probably gone to Newcastle and done the job, so the film's story was not as far-fetched as it might have seemed at the time. I married this story to the novel, which enabled me to give it a lot of texture. I'm not trying to say the book wasn't good in the first place – I thought it was terrific – but I was trying to give it yet another layer.

"It's ironic that Dryderdale Hall, previously the residence of Vincent Landa, should become the fictional home of the film's arch villain, Cyril Kinnear. It was a very spooky place; no one had wanted

to buy it, so we were able to use it. And we had to do very little to make it convincing. It was the real thing."

Child-on-ferry scene in Get Carter, *which was cut*

While searching for the locations Hodges was also thinking about a cinematographer. Dusty Miller had lit and operated *Rumour* but Klinger was nervous as Miller had never shot a feature film. Hodges then remembered seeing Ken Hughes' film *The Small World of Sammy Lee* (1963):

"It's a film that's been lost somewhere down the line. It starred Anthony Newley and Wilfred Brambell and, although I only saw it once, I remember being very impressed by it. So when I was asked to make *Get Carter*, I sought out the cameraman, Wolfgang Suschitsky, who had shot the film in black and white. He agreed to do it and Dusty generously agreed to be the operator. I'm not sure why that film stuck in my memory. Sammy Lee was a runt of a character, nothing like Jack Carter. But I remembered it had a kind of urgency and sleaziness. It was all shot in Soho. Ken Hughes is, in my opinion, a very under-estimated director and at the time I was a great fan of Anthony Newley.

"Obviously, while you want each of your films to be an original, it's impossible not to be influenced by films you've seen. As well as

The Small World of Sammy Lee I really liked Graham Greene's *Brighton Rock* (1947). Most of the other British crime films I'd seen weren't very impressive. They were unrealistic, soft. I wanted *Carter* to capture the ruthless viciousness revealed when the Krays and the Richardsons were finally brought to court. I wanted to be as honest as I could be with the original material but in fact ended up making a film much harder than the book."

Caine agrees with Hodges that making *Get Carter* was a chance to show gangsters as they really are and says he took the role of Jack Carter because he wanted to star in a truthful gangster picture: "I mean, compared with *Texas Chainsaw Massacre* it was *Mary Poppins*. But what was violent about it, was that the people were real. And so you believed the violence." Caine, of course, originates from the Elephant and Castle area of South London, which was, in his words, "a very rough district". With *Get Carter*, he liked the idea of telling it like it was:

"I'd always seen on screen, in British pictures, not American ones, gangsters were either stupid or very funny or Robin Hood types, stealing from the rich and giving to the poor. And I knew that none of these portraits were true. They weren't stupid and they were definitely not funny, they were very serious. Hodges knew that as well. He is a wonderful director because he takes things of the moment and if something is there that he can use, he'll use it. He's not rigid and all the best directors are never rigid. He was great. He came up with all sorts of new ideas once we'd got on location."

Until then Hodges had used mostly unknown actors in his films. "As I was also the producer no one ever asked me about the cast.

"Caine is Carter" film poster

They weren't obsessed with *names* like they are now. It was incredible. I was left completely to my own devices." Caine was the first film star he had encountered: *was* the advertising slogan, and it was right. He was Jack Carter. Like most actors established in the 1960s who came from his background, he knew this character

backwards. Everything he did was dead accurate. I'd always seen
Carter as a little seedier myself, but Michael simply stalked through
it, sharp as the Kray twins. He left the seediness to the people
around him. And luckily for me, when we got to shooting, Michael
was far more relaxed than other stars. He didn't expect to have a
close-up in every scene. Many stars would have been very pissed off
with the way I went about this film. But he knew he was in every
single scene and was savvy enough to realize that we didn't need the
traditional kind of coverage. In fact, in a lot of shots, I found myself
shooting whole sections on his back.

"When I was rehearsing my first scene with him, and this will
sound naïve, it suddenly dawned on me the difference between
working with ordinary actors and a star. I was looking through the
camera as he strode up the long bar to take the phone call from
Margaret. His head filled the screen, and I realized I was in a
completely different ball game. It wasn't to do with realism any

Left and right:
Caine as Carter set
a precedent for the
ultimate hard man
– gangsters have
never been cooler or
colder

longer, it was something else and I'm not sure I knew what it was – except that it was exciting."

Klinger and Hodges' instincts were right. Caine delivered a truly magnetic performance. His gripping portrayal of the hard-man hero out to avenge the recent murder of his brother is terrifying. He never forces a line, is completely confident and his calm, measured rhythms are ideally suited to the role. As Caine himself said at the time:

"Carter is a subtle combination of private eye and ruthless gangster. It's the strongest, most fascinating character I've played since Alfie. I modelled Carter on an actual hard case. I watched everything he did and once saw him put someone in hospital for 18 months. These guys are very polite but they act right out of the blue. They're not conversationalists about violence, they're perfectionists."

When it came to casting the rest of the film, MGM wanted to fill the screen with star names. This was not the way Hodges was used to working. He wanted to surround his star with believable

Hodges with camera operator Dusty Miller. They are lining up a shot of Carter watching a porn film from the bed

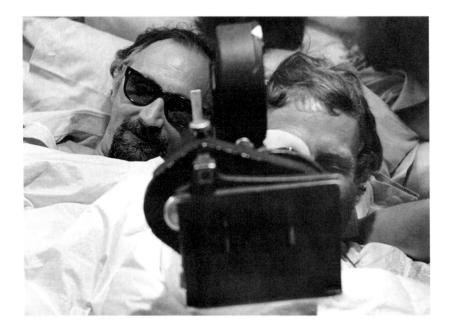

characters and could see all of his attempts at creating a realistic thriller flying out of the window.

"I thought that now we had a star on board I could complete the casting with actors of my choice. But to my astonishment, MGM

> "It's totally to do with instinct. You can smell a good actor. I rarely ask them to read. I just sit and talk with them, sometimes for a long, long time."
> Mike Hodges

kept coming up with these awful ideas such as Telly Savalas for the part of Cliff Brumby! They wanted 'names' even in the small characters. Personally I can't bear watching films with an audience waiting for the next big entrance and I fought hard not to let it happen here. I simply threatened to resign every time one of these ridiculous suggestions was made. In the end the only names we had on the marquee were Michael Caine and Britt Ekland who we cast as Carter's mistress. Britt solved the problem. Her name kept the producers happy, even if her role wasn't that big."

Another inspired piece of casting by Hodges and Irene Lamb, his casting director, was Ian Hendry. Hendry played the small but important role of Eric Paice, the seedy chauffeur to gang boss Cyril Kinnear (John Osborne). A decade earlier Hendry had been a much bigger name than Caine but by 1970 his career had waned, the result of bad choices, bad luck and a severe drink problem:

"Ian was a very heavy drinker and was really quite ill. I actually thought he was going to die on *Carter* during the chase sequence at the end of the film. His career was in tatters and he was extremely jealous of Caine. Ian was a terrific actor but simply wasn't destined to stay at the top whereas Michael obviously was. Maybe he didn't have the sex appeal? Maybe he simply wasn't dedicated enough to the idea of being a star? On the other hand Michael knew exactly how to go about becoming one and staying up there. When Ian arrived in Newcastle, I suggested we rehearse the racecourse scene where he meets Carter for the first time. He arrived at Michael's suite in the hotel completely pissed. It was chaos and so vitriolic. Michael handled the whole situation wonderfully. With Ian being abusive to him I just said, 'Forget it'. The next day, when they played the scene, it was just perfect. Inadvertently, I'd done the right thing because the clash between them has really got an edge to it. And it was meant."

The most difficult character to cast, according to Hodges, was Kinnear, the local godfather who, in Lewis's novel, was described as "very, very fat ... the kind of man that fat men like to stand next to. He had no hair and a handlebar moustache that made his face look a foot long on each side ... He was also only five foot two inches tall." Again Hodges was determined to go his own way and persuaded Michael Klinger to accept the writer John Osborne in the role. Osborne's controversial play *Look Back in Anger* had helped break down the conservative status quo in the mid-1950s. He had started as an actor and since his first play had written many major works for both theatre and cinema. However, unlike Kinnear in the novel, he was tall, slim and bearded.

In choosing the rest of the cast Hodges had his way, surrounding Caine with unknowns. He was back on his usual course:

"It's like a painter filling his canvas with characters. It's totally to do with instinct. You can smell a good actor. I rarely ask them to read. I just sit and talk with them, sometimes for a long, long time. I've noticed that American producers get terribly nervous when

> "I like to feel free of any preconceptions when I arrive on a set or location. I love flying from the seat of my pants. It's instinct again. There is just one moment when a scene comes together and, if you're relaxed enough as a filmmaker, you hope you will recognize it." Mike Hodges

they find out I don't do camera tests. Well, I'm paid for my instinct so that's what I rely on. Unfortunately some producers try to destroy your instinct, which begs the question of why on earth they employed you in the first place. Trouble is a lot of producers have no vision, no idea what they really want!"

Hodges used storyboards for complicated optical effects in *Flash Gordon* (1980) and the detailed surgical operation in *The Terminal Man* (1974), but in general hates the idea of using them:

"I like to feel free of any preconceptions when I arrive on a set or location. I love flying from the seat of my pants. It's instinct again. There is just one moment when a scene comes together and, if you're relaxed enough as a filmmaker, you hope you will recognize it. The worst thing you can do as a director is lay awake all night worrying about how you're going to shoot a scene, planning a complicated tracking shot or whatever, only to get on the set the next morning and realize there are three pillars and a sofa in the way! Better to sleep and arrive fresh. Hopefully that freshness will rub off on the scene.

"I like to retain the same sense of freedom with the sounds and music in my films. A sound man will always have his ears open for interesting sounds while we're on location. I always encourage this. Sounds, often unusual ones, can transform a scene. I love it when the sound editor offers you a selection of different, even surreal ones. Jim Atkinson, the sound editor on *Get Carter* was brilliant. Next time you see it listen for the little bells on the telephone sex scene. And when Jack knifes Albert Swift, listen for the distant ship's horn. It's a sad, soulful sound, like a dying elephant. It replaces Albert's last gasp.

"Sound tracks these days are too cluttered and noisy and there's far too much music. It always shows a director's insecurity. Actually it's more likely the producer who is nervous. Silence can make people very insecure. I have a theory that contemporary films have to be loud so audiences can't hear themselves eating."

Hodges soon discovered the importance of the first rushes that the studio executives see. If they're good, preferably sexy, they will feel secure and hopefully leave you alone, free of asinine suggestions. In the case of *Get Carter* he was lucky. The very first material they saw was the movie-within-the-movie footage. It was a porn movie. They loved it:

"The first material coming in from any film shoot is inevitably a surprise to film producers and financiers. It's rarely what they expect because it's hard, if not impossible, to visualize what it's

actually going to look like. If they're disappointed you've got problems from the off. With *Carter* I had the perfect lift-off. The pivotal moment in *Carter* is when Jack sees the porn film featuring his niece Doreen. Because I needed it for the actual scene I shot it in London before leaving for Newcastle. So – the first footage they ever saw was this tacky porn simulation. Perfect! They knew they were on to a winner. That says a lot about them, doesn't it? It's very important what you show these money men first.

"But it was embarrassing shooting it. We arrived at this prop man's house, where we were shooting it, a terraced house somewhere. There were three actresses, one actor and me. I had no idea how to start so we all sat in the lounge looking at each other. What made matters worse was the prop man's Alsatian had a big suppurating ulcer on its back and kept coming into the room. The whole experience was horrible. I had brought some champagne as a possible primer but funked producing it. Then one actress looked over at the small bar and says, 'I think I could do with a sherry.' So they all had a glass of this disgusting South African sherry and that did the trick. We started and it was finished in a couple of hours. It was my first and last pornographic film."

His first outing as director on a feature, Hodges impressed all concerned and ended up scripting, casting, directing and editing the entire movie, within its $750,000 budget, in just eight months.

Set in Newcastle c. 1970 in a world of gangland brutality, sex and corruption, Hodges begins as he means to go on, with a brilliant dreamy opening sequence, full of symbolism, which has Carter framed in a large picture window, up high in a penthouse apartment, alone, looking out at the night. There's hardly any light and already the viewer can sense death in the air. He turns away as the heavy satin curtains close, wiping him from view. His fate is sealed from the outset.

Next, in the opening credit sequence, Carter is on the train, reading a Raymond Chandler paperback, on his way to Newcastle for his brother Frank's funeral. It is only after watching the film a second time that some people will realize that Carter's eventual killer is sitting in the corner of the same carriage with him, already on his tail. The paperback is *Farewell, My Lovely*.

Previous page:
Caine, Hodges,
and Dorothy
White (Margaret)
at the
crematorium

Similarly, in a later scene set in a bingo hall, there's another one of Hodges' asides, in which he can't resist commenting on where the film is going. This time, as Carter walks into the hall, most of a management disclaimer notice above his head is obscured. All the lettering is excluded from the shot, apart from the words "The Game Is Final".

Get Carter is filled with these subtle touches and attention to detail: "I don't think anything should be stated obviously. I have always been obsessed by the detail in pictures," Hodges confesses.

The north-eastern setting is chillingly evoked. Although Carter has whisked himself away from his own soulless London surroundings, this city is equally drab and impersonal. As well as the grimy bingo hall, we see a world of seedy pubs, dingy local dance halls, dodgy boarding houses and grim back streets full of run-down row houses. The gangster film imagery is always present, from the sinister conveyer belt of black funeral cars pulling away as the family arrive for Frank's funeral, to the sudden explosions of violence as ugly as violence really is.

It doesn't take long for Jack Carter to suspect that his brother's

death wasn't an accident and he sets out with ruthless efficiency to find the man who ordered his execution. Shotgun in hand, he follows a seemingly never-ending trail of lies to find those responsible, uncovering a cesspool of corruption that's even tainted his innocent young niece (Petra Markham). Knowing the local criminal world, Carter looks around the racetrack and finds Cyril Paice (Hendry) a small-timer dressed up as a chauffeur. Following this trail brings him to a country house full of crooks headed by Roy Kinnear (Osborne). Although Carter is surprised to find himself more than welcome, he leaves with a warning to return to London before he causes any trouble. He ignores the warning and continues on his path of vengeance. With Carter now a loose cannon, a contract is put on his life.

The majorette sequence, which happened by pure chance

The shock ending is classic Hodges. Carter, having gleefully dispatched his brother's killer via a coal chute into the North Sea, strolls triumphantly along the sea front. He stops, looks at his shotgun, and decides to get rid of it. High on the cliff top a rifle and telescopic lens line up on him. A finger curls around the trigger. As

Carter goes to throw the murder weapon into the water, a shot rings out. Cue the waves gently lapping at Carter's lifeless body. This final sequence was shot on an overcast, murky day, making the event all the more bleak.

With its uncompromising violence and relentlessly grim atmosphere *Get Carter* was a sharp reflection of 1970s Britain, rife with industrial malaise and a world away from the fluffy 1960s. It was the gangster film that gave the genre a virulent dose of unremittingly bleak realism. In Newcastle Hodges had sensed the sickly smell of corruption that permeated the city. Without turning the film into a political statement, the social comment is there. Carter has become a criminal in order to live anywhere but the "crap house" where he was born. Newcastle is caught in transition, a city *Hodges and crew* on the cusp, one that is going to be irredeemably changed. The urban *on the streets of* tenements are in the process of being replaced by cold, inefficient *Newcastle* high-rise tower-block developments, funded by increasingly

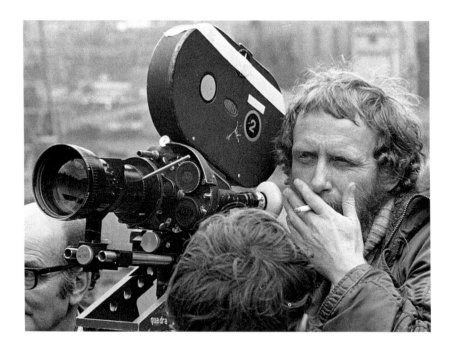

business-like crooks, men like Brumby. Not to mention the behind-closed-doors dealings of powerful drug-pedlars like Kinnear. Maybe *Get Carter* has survived and is more popular than ever because the film now fits more comfortably with the British people's view of their homeland?

"During my time in the navy and on *World in Action* I had a good look at the underbelly of Britain. I realized that despite the heritage image we liked to project it was as corrupt as any other country. Beneath the thatched image things were pretty rotten. Now, of course, it's there for all to see. There's no escape from it now but then there was. Once I'd decided to make *Carter*, I had to do it with the same ruthlessness as a surgeon opening up a cancer patient.

"I'm surprisingly sentimental about certain places in my life. For instance I find it painful going back to places I grew up in, particularly Salisbury, where I spent my childhood. Painful because they've changed almost out of recognition. Of course, most people living there are newcomers and unaware of this. But I am. And it's the same with Britain. I really should live somewhere else because watching what's happening here is too painful and it affects me badly. If I didn't care, or thought the changes were for the better, it wouldn't matter. But I do and they aren't.

"In *Carter* we see Brumby talking about his new restaurant, what it's going to be like. You've already seen his home so you know it's going to be shit. The man has no taste but he has money. That's the biggest change in this country. Pig ignorance and money are a lethal cocktail. Brumby represented, even then, the new Brit soon to come off the assembly line. Even the word 'Brit' is ugly!

"Interestingly, years after *Get Carter* I was asked to direct the BBC drama serial *Our Friends in the North*. I turned it down because in a way I was too obvious a choice. It was territory I'd already visited. At the time it occurred to me that *Carter* had caught the flavour of what was actually going on in Newcastle. It was only some years later that the extent of the corruption was finally exposed. I must have smelt it even then. Corruption does have a smell."

Hodges launched *Carter* into a world of sleaze, sex and decadence and succeeded in producing one of the finest and hardest-hitting portrayals of violence and corruption ever made. One year later, MGM remade it as a black exploitation movie set in LA. *Hit Man* (1972) starred Bernie Casey as the revenge-bent gunman trying to find out who killed his brother. But this remake had a happier ending, with the lead character narrowly escaping death at the end of the film.

A few years ago Hodges thought about doing another *Carter* film himself:

"I did write a synopsis but not based on any of the Ted Lewis novels. With Jack Carter dead I fantasized that he'd impregnated Anna. The boy is adopted by God-fearing parents who knew nothing of his genetic history. It was about the painful confusion of both the adoptive parents and the child now as psychotic and violent as his father. I wanted to journey with the young Jack as he discovers the facts of his father's life. Is he trapped in a genetic prison and, if he is, can he escape? I've recently read John Pearson's second book on the Kray twins, *The Cult of Violence*. It's brilliant and one can understand and even sympathize with the genetic trap they were in. I sent the

treatment to Warner Bros. who own the rights to *Carter*. Needless to say it was rejected. A remake with Stallone was already in the works but I didn't know it."

In 2000 Sylvester Stallone starred in Stephen Kay's completely watered-down version. It also had Michael Caine cast in the supporting role of Cliff Brumby (originally played by Bryan Mosley), and he got to be on the other side of his most famous line from the original film: "You're a big man, but you're out of shape. With me it's a full time job. Now behave yourself." Not surprisingly, however, Stallone's remake drew terrible reviews and bombed at the box office. In fact, critics were not even given a chance to attend preview screenings, which meant that the weekly entertainment guides around the US had no chance to warn cinema-goers just how bad the movie was. Later, however, in a review that appeared in the

New York Times, Elvis Mitchell wrote: "It's so minimally plotted that not only does it lack context and subtext but it also may be the world's first movie without even a text." He reported audience members filing out within half an hour of the film starting. Hodges obviously expressed his disappointment: "I don't know why they decided to remake it. For the amount of money spent on it they could have made plenty of original films. Remakes signal death of the imagination. I just wish they hadn't used the same title."

It does seem crazy that such a numbing mishmash of a movie can get made. The only positive aspect of the whole affair is that, hopefully, reviewers will have pointed out how much better the original film is and drawn Hodges' *Get Carter* to the attention of a new generation of filmgoers.

Looking at the film now, more than 30 years on, it's noticeable how it hasn't dated at all. Through the clever use of costumes by designer Vangie Harrison, *Get Carter* will always look contemporary. And it will always remain cool, thanks to Caine's performance, Roy Budd's minimalist soundtrack, and Hodges' direction.

A seminal British thriller, *Get Carter* redefined the genre for British moviemakers. Its influence on British filmmaking can be seen from *The Long Good Friday* (1981) to recent Brit flicks such as *Lock, Stock and Two Smoking Barrels* (1999), *Snatch* (2000), *Face* (1997), *Gangster No 1* (2000) and *Love, Honour and Obey* (2000).

The film industry's current man of the moment, Guy Ritchie, says he made *Lock, Stock* and *Snatch* because he felt nothing much had been done with the genre in the UK for a long time, and he thought he could exploit it to make a name for himself. But even though Ritchie claims he's not a fan of most British gangster films, he does have a soft spot for *Get Carter*. "It was stylish, it had an identity – Michael Caine at his best," he says. "It was a grown-up film. My favourite bit in the film was when Caine was coming out naked with a shotgun and a northern military band was going by outside – he didn't give a toss. It was one of those quirky, good scenes."

Get Carter was the original – and the best – British gangster movie. A truly great film is one that stands the test of time and can still touch people long after the hype is gone. *Get Carter* was recently named the

16th top British film of all time in a BFI poll. It was also voted the best British film of all time by *Hotdog* magazine and hailed as a timeless classic by *Loaded* magazine, which serialized the movie in cartoon form. *Loaded*'s celebration of *Get Carter* was one of the main factors which helped push the main character of the film back to the centre of attention in the 1990s, although Hodges was not overjoyed that Jack Carter has became an icon of "Lad culture": "I absolutely loathe it and who wouldn't? I hate Lad culture. It's a mindless macho culture with neo-fascist undertones. They even have the uniforms. Do we really want to live in a world filled with male slobs?"

On its initial release *Get Carter* received very mixed reviews with many critics denouncing its violence. Felix Barker of *The Evening News* described Hodges' film as "a succession of gratuitously sadistic and titillating scenes", and Cecil Wilson of the *Daily Mail* asked, "Did it have to be quite so gratuitously brutal?" But in the *Daily Express*, Ian Christie wrote: "The result is a tremendously exciting thriller that gives Michael Caine the best part he has had in years. Carter, you will gather, is not a nice person to know … It is a cruel, vicious film, even allowing for its moments of humour, but completely compelling nevertheless. I'd get Carter if I were you. It certainly got me."

Get Carter shocked audiences in 1971 and still carries an 18 certificate today. Although recently revered as the ultimate celebration of cool 1970s' machismo, an expression of cold British laddish values, to reclaim the film in this way is to miss the point. It is possible that *Get Carter* still frightens people, not because there is blood and gore or much in-your-face physical violence, but because of the underlying themes. Viewers may be frightened to look beyond the punch-ups and phone sex.

Get Carter certainly is a great film, and can obviously be enjoyed as a piece of entertainment but it is also a film which reeks of despair, emptiness and death. Some critics view it as an urban western, with Caine as the stranger riding into town, loaded with his own private anger and out for revenge. But *Get Carter* is closer to the Jacobean revenge drama, with the Caine character more reminiscent of the Mifune character in Kurosawa's *Yojimbo* (1961) or the unstoppable, incorruptible samurai leader in *Seven Samurai* (1954). The Caine

character is implacable and elemental, like Vindici in Middleton's revenge drama *Revengers Tragedy*, and in the end he has to die.

As in Hodges' earlier television dramas, death is ever present. Carter's quest leaves a litter of corpses. But then, if there is one key underlying theme throughout the films of Mike Hodges, it is both the certainty – and uncertainty – of death. Later in his career came the deeply unsettling *The Terminal Man* (1974), about a computer scientist (George Segal) who becomes homicidal during periodic blackouts. In the acclaimed *Black Rainbow* (1990) Hodges explores not only death but the idea of a constant recycling of the life force; and in the more recent *Croupier* (1998) we are reminded of how life and death are as much to do with chance as anything else. Films as dark as this don't often make it into the mainstream movie circuit. But perhaps viewers are afraid to participate in Hodges' observations on the randomness of the world and the lives of its inhabitants.

*A sundeck that
proved an
unnecessary luxury*

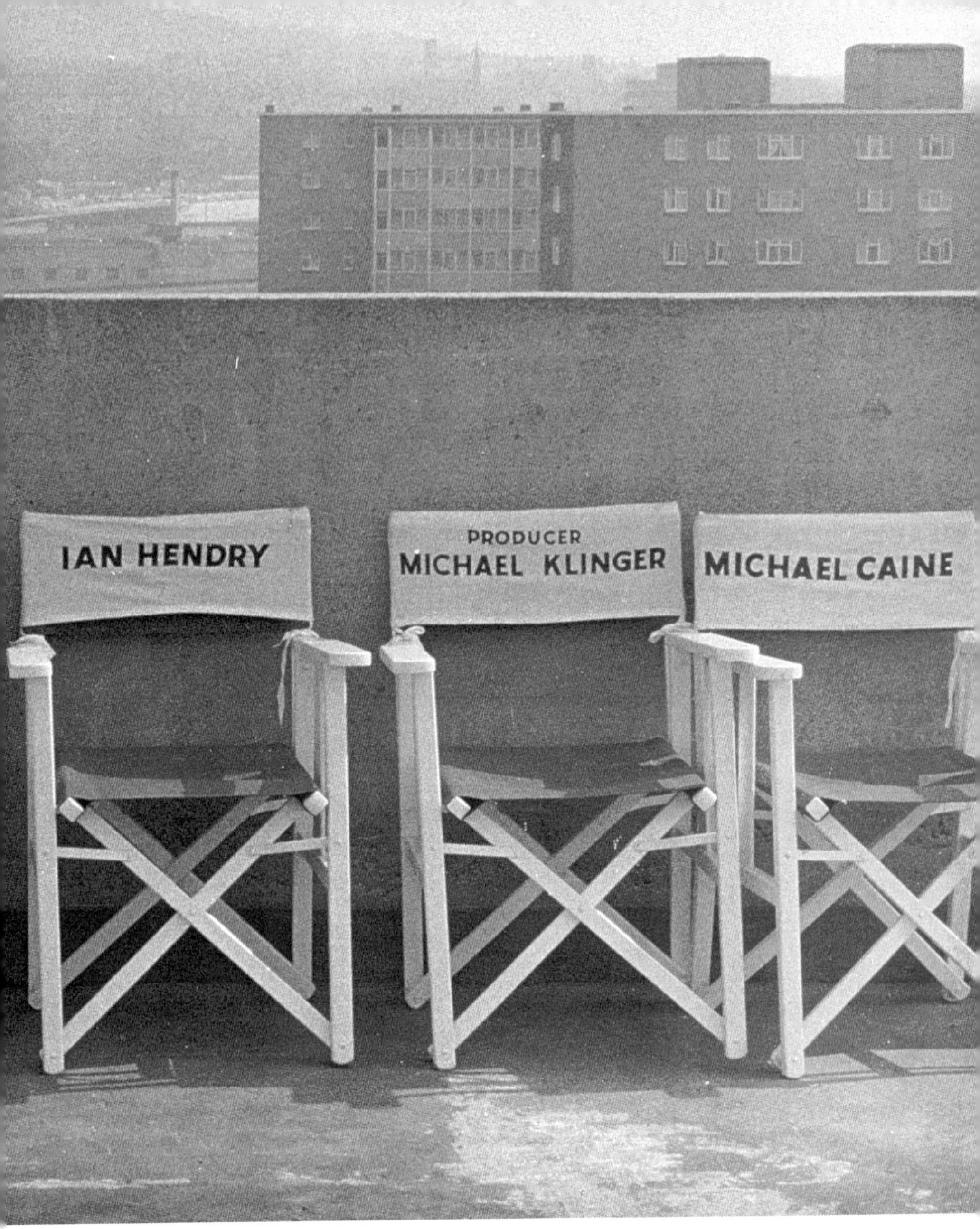
IAN HENDRY
PRODUCER
MICHAEL KLINGER
MICHAEL CAINE

Unlike *Villain* (1971) and *The Krays* (1990), Hodges' *Get Carter* isn't a formulaic, studio-style picture made by committees. It is a superbly structured revenge thriller that was written and directed by one man. An *auteur* film, it was undoubtedly way ahead of its time and will easily survive beyond the ironic appreciation of the *Loaded* generation. As Jack Carter, Michael Caine was a cold, brutal and methodical assassin – a world away from the average macho British "lad". At the moment, current hip gangster films such as *Lock, Stock* and *Face* offer nothing more than pure entertainment with no social detail. They are farces, something to laugh at. Hodges' groundbreaking classic, however, will always be a film to be taken seriously.

Taking on the Gangsters: Pulp

"Where *do* you get your ideas from, Mickey?"
Princess Betty Cippola in *Pulp*

Chapter 3

Mike Hodges was surprised, even alarmed, at the audience reaction to *Get Carter*. Previously, having only directed movies for television, he'd never witnessed a live audience reacting to any of his films. But with *Get Carter*, Hodges found himself in the middle of a packed screening at the Odeon in Leicester Square, London:

"I could hear every reaction, feel the excitement. They were hooked. They gasped and laughed on cue. It was heady stuff all right, but I found it unnerving. I hadn't anticipated the sense of power you can get as a director. It was Pavlovian and I found that scary. The other dichotomy for me was the audience hadn't reacted as I'd expected. I was expecting people to be shocked, even disgusted, but they weren't. Most of them had a good time with it. They were exhilarated.

"Looking back the whole experience was bizarre. Women looked at me differently, or was it in my imagination? Was it because of the telephone sex scene? Friends seemed to look at me differently too. They couldn't believe the small, gentle, laughing man they knew could make such a film! It was an awful shock to a lot of people, including my parents although they never said so. Even to this day the farmer who lives up the road from me asks how could I have possibly made such a vile picture!"

In response to these reactions Hodges wrote and directed a 30-minute drama for London Weekend Television called *The Manipulators* (1971). It's a film about emotional manipulation, with most of the action taking place in one room. It opens with a delivery man dropping off meat carcasses to a butcher's shop. Inside the walk-in refrigerator the man changes places with another agent who has come from the flat above. We know we are into a surveillance operation. The victim, David Stanley (Alexander Morton who had a small role in *Get Carter* and later as the casino manager in *Croupier*) is a psychology student. He lives with his wife and child across the street. The two agents record their every move. Worse, they are watching how they react to anonymous calls, fake phone messages and a letter from a fictitious lover. We see Stanley attending a lecture on Pavlov with film of the famous dog experiments. We see his wife at a typing college acquiring the skill by rote. Events take a more horrific turn: when Stanley's jealous anger explodes (he appears to

Previous page: Lizabeth Scott (Princess Betty Cippola) with Robert Sacchi (Bogeyman) in Mike Hodges' surreal black comedy Pulp *(1972)*

actually kill his wife and child), one of the agents shows his horrified disgust. They have gone too far. Then, completely unexpectedly, it's revealed that the whole operation had been a test for the unsuspecting agent. And because *he* failed, it is *he* who must be killed. He was too human.

Like *Get Carter*, *The Manipulators* is cold, seedy and unsettling, with a brilliant final twist. As in so many of Hodges' films the end is in the beginning. Another delivery van arrives; only this time a carcass is taken away. A human one.

Hodges' half-hour drama is a disturbing piece examining how easily we can be manipulated. How our minds are constantly being messed with. Of course, ultimately it is Hodges who has been messing with minds. The viewers of this excellent little drama have been manipulated. Perhaps, if producers are so keen to do remakes, they should look to clever stories such as this one.

After the success of *Get Carter* Hodges was being offered all kinds of film projects. "I think Michael Caine was a bit miffed that, in the wake of *Carter*'s success, I chose to do a half-hour television drama!" recalls Hodges. "But I love doing 25-minute films like *The Manipulators*. The form can be perfect, like a jewel. Something a feature film can rarely be. They usually sprawl."

Not surprisingly producer Michael Klinger was eager to work with Hodges and Caine again. Klinger, Caine and Hodges formed their own company. At first they called it 3M. Then the giant 3M Corporation contacted and they changed it to the Three Michaels.

Hodges had a project in mind especially tailored for Caine. He wrote it on spec not wanting the strait-jacket of a commission. Six months later he finished the first draft, hoping his new partners would like it. They did, and so did United Artists. That's how *Pulp* came to be made:

"I wanted to make a comedy. People don't see *Carter* as a film with comic elements but it does have a lot of funny moments, even though the humour is wickedly black. So having made a very hard thriller I actually became addicted to hearing audiences laugh. I love making people laugh anyway and now wanted to do it in the cinema. In a way I wanted to do something light, as a bookend to *Carter*, to get away from the violence. Mind you, my humour might be described as very surreal and rather bleak.

"So I began working on a story, originally called *Memoirs of a Ghostwriter*, which I later changed to *Pulp*. It's always hard to remember exactly the genesis of a script, what was that first idea. In the case of *Pulp* I think it was when I read about a surge in the neo-fascist vote in the Italian local elections. I was horrified by this. I had assumed, again naïvely, that fascism had been eliminated for ever in World War II. Hadn't we all seen the horrors of the concentration camps? At the age of 13 I'd kept a cuttings album of the newspaper photographs and swore I would never ever speak to a German. But Italian fascists had always seemed comic, operatic, not sinister like the Nazis. Anyway I think that's where I started.

"This element somehow became attached to a scandal I remembered in Italy in the 1950s. It was dubbed the Montesi Scandal, a *cause célèbre* in its time, in which a young girl was found dead on a beach. The case shook the foundations of the Italian government and, as only could happen in Italy, it rolled on and on, and the investigations eventually lasted for over a decade. Over the years numerous people were arrested for the murder, then acquitted. There were endless court trials where the great and the good were

> "It's always hard to remember exactly the genesis of a script, what was that first idea. In the case of *Pulp* I think it was when I read about a surge in the neo-fascist vote in the Italian local elections."
> Mike Hodges

put on the witness stand. Even fortune tellers would be brought in to give their views. The Pope and the Catholic Church somehow got involved and it just went on and on. It was fodder for the popular press and the mix of sex and scandal fed the fantasies of people all over the world for a long time. I don't think to this day anyone's found out what actually happened. This became the spine of the plot.

"Klinger agreed to finance a research trip to Italy. I went to

Predappio in the north and visited Benito Mussolini's tomb. It was bombed, I think, some years later. In the town I found a shop which illegally sold photos of Il Duce, postcards and even LPs of his speeches. Fascism was certainly alive and well in Italy. At the end of *Pulp* you'll see there's a jukebox outside Mickey Rooney's mausoleum. It's almost exactly the same as the one in front of Mussolini's tomb where you could actually push buttons to hear segments from his speeches.

"Another element floating around in my mind was a memory of the gangster star George Raft coming to London. For a while he worked as a greeter in a casino. He'd been kicked out of America for supposed Mafia connections. Why that stuck in my memory I'll never know. Anyway these were the ingredients in my mental Magimix when I was writing *Pulp*."

Caine with Lionel Stander in Pulp

With all this in mind, *Pulp*, not surprisingly, is full of Mafia references and covered-up scandals, a bewildering chain of events involving an extraordinary off-beat group of characters. Caine is Mickey King, a tacky pulp fiction writer who's earned a living of sorts with titles such as *My Gun is Long* and *The Organ Grinder*, using pseudonyms such as O R Gan, S Odomy, Les Behan, Paul R Cumming and Guy Strange.

King, who also narrates the story, is enjoying carefree tax exile in the Mediterranean. But this turns into something resembling one of his bad plots when Ben Dinuccio (Lionel Stander) approaches him to ghost write the memoirs of a mystery celebrity now living in retirement on a Mediterranean island. Encouraged by his agent Marcovic (Leopoldo Trieste) he accepts and finds himself travelling with a coach party, waiting to meet his "contact" who will lead him to his mystery client.

He is convinced it's Miller (Al Lettieri), an American who strikes up a conversation with him on the coach. But Miller quickly shies off when King suggests business and, at the hotel where their rooms are changed in a mix-up, King finds Miller lying in a bath of blood in the room that should have been his.

But next morning there is no fuss, no police, no questions. The hotel tells King that Miller checked out early. King continues on the coach tour still wondering about the identity of his contact. Is it the mystery Englishman (Dennis Price) who delights in quoting Lewis Carroll? Or the severe-looking nun? No – it is the shapely Liz Adams (Nadia Cassini) whose sugar daddy is the mystery celebrity. He is the faded Hollywood film star Preston Gilbert (Mickey Rooney) who specialized in gangster roles and whose connection with the mob was more than academic.

Growing increasingly nervous King travels with Liz and Ben Dinuccio to Gilbert's private island. The over-the-hill noir star turns out to be a foulmouthed, obnoxious, abusive little man with a very twisted sense of humour.

With the job complete the two sail to the mainland for a party to celebrate the end of the book. Here King meets Princess Betty Cippola (Lizabeth Scott) a former wife of Gilbert and now married to a neo-fascist politician (Victor Mercieda), leader of the New Front, a party that's big on law and order. Gilbert is famous for his bad-taste practical jokes one of which is posing as a waiter, and spilling food and wine on unsuspecting customers. He goes into the well-worn routine, only this time the joke misfires. Suddenly King finds life mirroring one of his "pulps" when Gilbert is gunned down by a mysterious priest. Trouble is the priest then starts gunning for him, too.

After a narrow escape, and now back on the island, King learns from Dinuccio that somebody, a prominent somebody, involved in a sex scandal with Gilbert had got wind of the proposed biography. King is bound to be the next target. Now desperate, King seeks out a clairvoyant Gilbert had been consulting. The man gives him a faded picture of a hunting party group and a newspaper photo of a dead girl.

At Gilbert's lavish funeral King realizes all of the mourners are members of the hunting party in the photo. Leaving the funeral he seeks out a contact in a deserted town where a one-armed man takes him to a grave on a lonely beach. The pieces start to fit together. A burst of gunfire heralds a black-clad figure descending on King, machine-gun blazing. King and his guide crawl towards their battered truck, bullets puncturing the sand all around them. Starting the truck King turns it towards the man, closing on him.

It is the priest.

He drives straight for him, knocking him flat. The one-armed man collapses and falls from his seat of the truck, dead. King walks over to the body of the priest. "That costume might just get you through those pearly gates," he says, "but I doubt it." Then he eulogizes over the corpse: "Remember that thou art pulp, and unto pulp thou shalt return – a fitting epitaph for Jack Francis Miller, priest, lecturer and drag queen."

King has also been hit by a bullet. His wounded leg lands him not in hospital but as the unwilling guest of Cippola, the leader of the New Front party. A prisoner in his palace, King spends his time working on his latest tacky masterpiece. He reads the proofs aloud to the assembled house party: "I slammed my fist into his face as hard as I could. There was the sound of crunching bones. Blood splattered everywhere like a burst water main. But the blood wasn't red, it was blue. I swung round and found myself looking at Prince Cippola…".

Princess Cippola interrupts: "Where do you get your ideas from?" she asks as she leaves.

King looks at the camera defiantly: "I'll get the bastards yet!" he exclaims, and then with even more conviction, "Ooh, I wish my leg didn't itch."

Having devised a wonderfully unique story, Hodges admits that the process of writing *Pulp* was not an easy one:

"I found it hard because it was always pushing believability to the limit. I was also having fun with coincidences, taking them full on. My other scripts had quite straightforward narratives, whereas with *Pulp* I was trying something new. I admit to being much influenced by the John Huston film *Beat the Devil* (1954), a marvellous movie with Gina Lollobrigida, Peter Lorre and Humphrey Bogart, full of weird, witty scenes. I had loved that film. It had died at the box office. At the time I was the only person I knew who had seen it. It was written on the hoof by Truman Capote. He didn't find it easy either.

"With *Pulp*, I wanted a totally new creative team. I was making a different film to *Get Carter*. Weirdly the content was much the same, corruption at the top and the abuse of a young woman, but the style was to be very different! So I decided to have a different cinematographer, designer, editor, composer and costume designer. For all of them (with the exception of wonderful Git Magrinni – the costume designer on *Il Conformista*) it was a first cinema film.

> "Mickey was strange. We never once talked about his character. He just showed up, put his wardrobe on and delivered the lines, brilliantly. I had written Gilbert as a pretty monstrous character, but Mickey somehow made him even more monstrous!" Mike Hodges

Ousama Rawi and I had worked on commercials together, as I had with the editor. The designer, Pat Downing, had worked on my television films *Suspect* and *Rumour*."

Originally, *Pulp* was to have been shot in Italy because the back-

Mickey Rooney as over-the-hill noir star Preston Gilbert

story stemmed from what was happening there. But when the location manager went to fix the locations chosen by Hodges, at every one he found himself having to make a deal with the Mafia. The irony of this, bearing in mind the content of the script, didn't go unnoticed. Hodges, fearing "they were being taken to the cleaners", phoned Klinger and asked if it could be shot somewhere else, and suggested Malta. Hodges had a house there and knew the island well. The film was shot there in the winter of 1971/2. With only four weeks to the start date the production manager and costume designer came over from Italy and the rest of the crew flew in later from the UK.

"We were filming in Malta at the time the British were being kicked out by the Prime Minister, Dom Mintoff," Michael Klinger remembers. "There were lots of stories in the paper about it, never true. We became very friendly with Mintoff, a tough little man who gave us a lot of help."

On one occasion journalist Jack Bentley of the *Sunday Pictorial* called Klinger in search of a story and asked how the cast and crew were spending their spare time. Klinger told him they were off to play football against a local team and he was welcome to cover that if he wanted. The match wasn't a great success: "I was the referee," said Klinger, "Michael Caine was the linesman and our secret weapon was Stanley Matthews who had gone to live on Malta. We still lost 6–0."

Malta was a location Caine took a dislike to and made a mental note never to visit again. When an interviewer from the BBC World Service asked what he liked most about the island, Caine's reply was instant: "The plane home." He didn't like the island or the people and later explained: "I adore trees and gardens, and Malta is the only land I've ever been to that has no trees. It drove me bananas!"

According to Hodges, the rest of the cast enjoyed their stay in Malta:

"We had a great time. Malta was the perfect place to shoot. I thoroughly enjoyed it but then I was working with some terrific actors. Actors like Rooney, Scott, Stander, Dennis Price, people I'd dreamt of working with one day.

"Mickey Rooney was extraordinary. I had a real fight with United Artists to get him approved. The character had to be short like Mussolini and Hitler, and also like many gangster stars, Cagney for example. A lot of the jokes stemmed from Gilbert's size. Rooney was out of fashion in those days, but I insisted he was the only person to play the part. UA were coming up with all sorts of insane suggestions. The craziest was Victor Mature. I had to point out that he was over 6 foot tall. I began to wonder if they'd read the script.

"Mickey was strange. We never once talked about his character. He just showed up, put his wardrobe on and delivered the lines, brilliantly. I had written Gilbert as a pretty monstrous character, but Mickey somehow made him even more monstrous! I quickly realized I had to shoot even the rehearsals because he'd never do the same thing twice. The freshness would soon evaporate and he'd become mechanical. It was very exhausting for a director to deal with that. When I was trying to match close-ups with other actors, he'd be tap-dancing or pretending to play the drums.

"Lizabeth Scott was equally tiring for me, but in a different way. She hadn't made a movie for about 15 years and I really had to coax her into coming back. She was very nervous. In the first scene I shot with her she was holding a cup and saucer. You could hear them rattling she was shaking so badly. Her confidence constantly needed firing up. But I loved her voice and having her in the film reminded me of those classic Hollywood gangster films I loved. She was terrific in it."

Hodges had tailored the part of Mickey King for Michael Caine as he explains:

"In *Get Carter*, we were shooting a scene in which he drove a car. I said to my first assistant, 'Right – ask Michael to get in and drive off.'

There had been a stunned silence and Johnny Morris, Michael's man, took me aside and whispered, 'Michael doesn't drive.'

'Doesn't drive?' I said. 'But he played Alfie – a chauffeur!'

'Yes, but he was towed everywhere,' Johnny replied.

So when I wrote *Pulp* there's a scene when Michael is chased by a gunman across a beach. The guy who drove him there is gunned down and his last words to Michael are, 'Can you drive?'

'No,' says Michael, as the van kangaroos across the beach!"

Hodges' biggest problem on *Pulp* was the editing. The original editor was, sadly, treating the material too reverently. "He was making an 'art' film – which I certainly wasn't," recalls Hodges. "I struggled to bring him around, but to no avail. It was the first time I'd ever had to fire somebody. I hated doing it."

Klinger knew an editor called John Glen (later the director of the Bond movies of the 1980s) and hired him to take over. Glen joined Hodges and the pair started from scratch. At the time, Britain was in the grip of industrial unrest and Glen knew there wasn't much time:

"We were restricted by a three-day week and the electricity supply was prone to disappear without warning. When the lights went out, there was nothing else for it but to head for the pub because there was no way to get any work done."

Hodges asked Glen how long it would take to edit the film. "At this rate," replied Glen, "at least a month."

"Mike is a nice guy and I admired his work enormously, so I took the job. But the film had been hacked around a bit," recalls Glen. "I had to have the whole lot put back to rushes so I could start again.

"I thought the end result was quite amusing, but I had a problem with the fact that Mickey Rooney's character got assassinated half way through. Mickey was a real live wire, and the film missed him desperately. It was interesting to see Lizabeth Scott, who I remembered seeing in films when I was a kid, and Lionel Stander was wonderful. Michael Caine did a great job, of course."

John Glen is right. Michael Caine did do a fine job. His gift for light comedy has never been better used. His Spillane-style voice-over narration is just perfect. Voice-over is notoriously difficult to pull off without it becoming divorced from the visuals. Although

Michael Caine as pulp-fiction writer Mickey King

recorded many months after the shooting was finished, Caine is still Mickey King, the seedy, desperate, tacky ghost writer. He did it brilliantly.

Producer Michael Klinger agreed that Hodges had delivered a fine film, saying, "We've made this for 1975. I'm a man who looks ahead. I don't like to follow trends, I like to set them."

At the time of its release in 1972, *Pulp* received mainly good reviews, but failed to make an impression at the box office. This could be explained by the film's rather curious opening in the US. It was given the red carpet treatment in, of all places, Philadelphia. W C Fields wanted on his tombstone: "Better here than Philadelphia", so he would have found it funny. The film died. However, soon afterwards, a new cinema opened in New York, dedicated to showing "lost" films. The venue chose *Pulp* as its first title, to run for one week only. The reviews were brilliant, with *Time* magazine calling it a "minor masterpiece". Sadly, these came out as – or after – the film had closed. "The distributors rushed around trying to find venues," recalls Hodges, "but by then the window had closed."

After realizing the new 3M film had not matched the commercial success of *Get Carter*, Michael Klinger was quoted as saying: "Hodges finished the whole thing in mid-air. That's how it is in real life but not how you finish a movie. At the end people felt cheated, but the critics loved it."

Of those critics in the UK, Ian Christie of the *Daily Express* praised the performances: "The commentary by Michael Caine is wryly funny, and there is a splendidly extravagant performance by Rooney." Meanwhile, *Time* magazine's Jay Cocks wrote: "Hodges has not only got his distance in *Pulp*, he has also found a style and voice of his own. He is constantly, ebulliently inventive, whether in scrupulously outrageous dialogue or in one of the many dazzling visual jokes."

Although this film hasn't been distributed much on video or DVD, it is certainly worth seeing. "All the writers I know seem to love *Pulp* for some reason, including, I learnt recently, J G Ballard. What with the rise of Le Pen and Berlusconi the film has a certain prescience. In fact Berlusconi looks rather like Cippola," explains Hodges.

With Mike Hodges back in fashion, thanks to *Croupier*, perhaps people will take the opportunity to revisit this spiky comedy. *Pulp* is the perfect antidote to the brutality of Hodges' seminal gangster film *Get Carter*. It is nostalgic, funny, satirical and very clever. It also again highlights Hodges' views on power, corruption and politics. The film's chief strength, though, is not a particular star, but the way Hodges' direction knits everything into one audacious whole, full of fire and wit. It puts most of today's comic movies to shame.

After *Pulp*, in the winter of 1972, came the call from Hollywood...

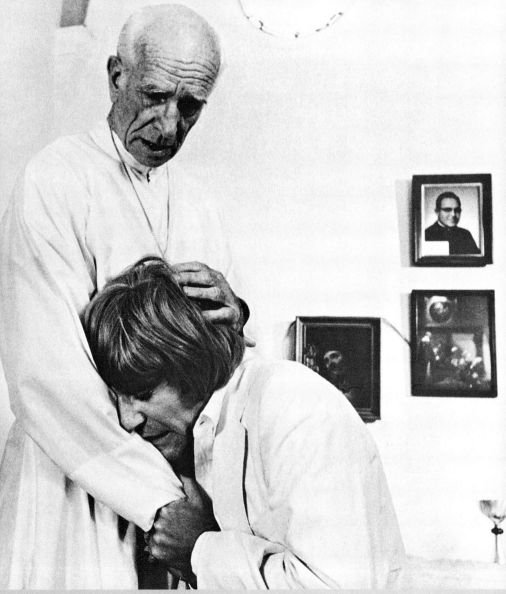

Mind Control:
The Terminal Man

Chapter 4

"A film is – or should be – more like music than
like fiction. It should be a progression of moods and
feelings. The theme, what's behind the emotion, the
meaning, all that comes later."
Stanley Kubrick

When Hodges had finished editing *Pulp*, he took his family – in a
Land Rover – to North Africa, for a long holiday. On his return, in
the pile of mail waiting for him, was a letter from Warner Bros'
John Calley, together with a copy of Michael Crichton's novel *The
Terminal Man.*

Calley wanted Hodges to adapt, produce and direct the novel,
a story about a brilliant computer scientist called Harry Benson,
who, as the result of a head injury, begins to experience violent
seizures and occasional bouts of uncontrollable rage.

After reading the book and a meeting with Calley in London,
Hodges accepted and in January 1973, he left for Los Angeles.
Having always been interested in working in Hollywood, he was
anxious to see what it would be like – but there was a problem.
About to embark on his most dangerous mission to date – his first
Hollywood feature – he was suffering from severe depression.

"It had been building up for a while and the holiday hadn't really
helped. I was going through hell and wasn't stable at all. I was in a
situation where I was married, had two kids at private school, a

*Previous page:
The Terminal
Man's Catholic
hero Harry Benson
(George Segal)
turns to religion for
help (Ian Wolfe is
the priest)*

*Below: Out of
control, Benson
strangles the priest*

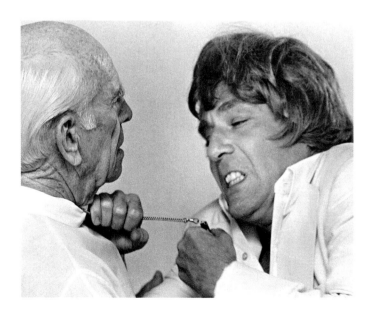

house in London, a house in the country, two cars, everything that we needed – and I just loathed it. My depression, I think, all stemmed from realizing how I'd ended up. It's not what I'd intended, as I'm not a materialist in that sense.

"Nevertheless, when I was sent the book I was drawn to it, even though it was dangerous territory for a man who was seriously depressed.

"Anyway I went to Los Angeles and immediately hated it. In fairness I simply didn't know anybody there. The studio put me in the Beverly Hills Hotel and I quickly ended up like Harry, the lead character in the film. I used to think my head was going to explode and I would be rocking on the floor of my luxury suite, unable to leave. I could hear people going by, on their way to breakfast, but I couldn't bring myself to leave my room. When I did go out, I'd face other terrifying scenarios, like driving. There's no escape from driving in LA. I rang the rental company and asked for a small car. When I finally plucked up the courage to go down to the hotel's garage I found that they had delivered this mother of a car which, compared to my Mini back home, was like a tank!"

In a complete state of confusion and disintegration, Hodges was becoming alarmingly like the lead character in the movie he was supposed to be producing and directing. And although he had previously tried to work through his problems with a psychiatrist, he didn't find the process much use. Instead, Hodges managed to hold on to his sanity by constantly photographing the contents of his hotel room. "Looking through a camera helps with vertigo. I know. I suffer from vertigo." Taking the reality out of his situation, he made himself treat life like watching a film, seeing everything through a small square box. Hodges took pictures of anything and everything. More than once, he recalls sitting on the toilet, taking pictures of his trousers around his ankles. He'd also take photographs of his breakfast tray, the television set, the hotel bathroom, anything that was around him.

By looking through the view finder of his camera, Hodges was somehow able to hang on and make some sort of sense of his personal predicament. While initial attempts at defining himself within his new LA world resulted in feelings of uncertainty and anxiety, these feelings eventually gave rise to a simultaneous responsibility to have to create something in place of that emptiness.

"A magnificent, overwhelming picture … achieves moods that I've never experienced in the movies before"
Terrence Malick on *The Terminal Man*

When Hodges came out of the depression and managed to focus on his life and current project, his breakdown ultimately became a breakthrough. Luckily, he got through the general Hollywood mayhem and insanity and did a great job. Hodges' own isolation and loneliness provided the basis for the whole mood of the film. While Hodges was being "looked after" by his agents and the studio in *The Terminal Man*, Harry Benson found himself in the hands of cold, unfeeling medics.

Much of the film is concerned with the attitudes of those who treat Benson, a group of aloof, shallow individuals who treat patients like machinery to be mended. Brilliantly played by George Segal, Harry Benson volunteers for revolutionary treatment and is implanted with a "lympic brain-pacing device", a kind of microcomputer, which sends tiny electric shocks to the brain to neutralize his violent seizures whenever they occur.

Head surgeon, Dr Ellis (Richard Dysart) and doctors Ross (Joan Hackett), Morris (Michael C Gwynne) and McPherson (Donald Moffat) successfully carry out the operation and place Benson under 24-hour guard while they monitor its effect. Dr Ross and electronics technician Gerhard (Matt Clark) test the implant by using it to stimulate the various pleasure, emotion and pain centres of Benson's brain. In this disturbing scene, Dr Ross sits interviewing him while, behind a mirrored window, the technicians activate the various implant nodes. They go from making him feel like he's just tasted a ham sandwich to having him feel the desperate urge to urinate, as well as inducing various childhood memories. The doctors induce a seizure under clinical surroundings and prove that the implant prevents it from overwhelming the patient.

However, the seizures begin to increase in frequency. The doctors realize that Benson's brain has become addicted to the electric shocks and is actually triggering the seizures to obtain more stimulation. Driven by the addictive need, he escapes the hospital and takes refuge with his girlfriend Angela Black (Jill Clayburgh). The doctors think his next seizure will be in a few hours and, sure enough, Benson is suddenly seized with another attack. He grabs a pair of scissors and stabs his lover to death.

Before the operation, Benson takes questions from medics about his rare condition

With the tiny computer in his brain malfunctioning at an increasingly greater rate, Benson is transformed into a pitiful, rampaging monster, a modern-day Frankenstein set loose in Los Angeles. During his next seizure, he breaks into his old laboratory to destroy a robot he was working on before his injury, and later he attacks and kills a priest whom he'd gone to for help.

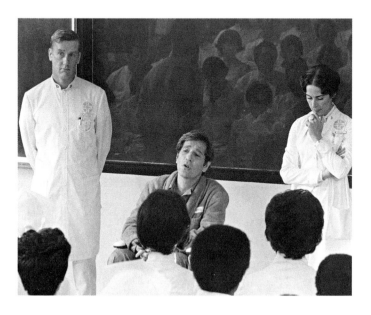

Dr Ross has gone home to rest. She is notified of these latest events just as she hears Benson's voice downstairs in her home. She panics and tries to talk him into going back to the hospital. As another seizure comes over him, Dr Ross stabs him. He flees, mortally wounded, to a nearby graveyard and deliberately jumps into an open grave. It's a place where he can do no more harm. Dr Ross is brought to the scene by the police. As she tries to talk him into giving himself up, a police helicopter arrives. Benson raises his handgun in defiance and a sharpshooter from the helicopter above shoots him dead.

Segal as the helpless pawn

The film ends as it started with the police helicopter. At the start it is taking off, at the end it is landing. A lot has happened in between.

To this day, George Segal maintains the Harry Benson character is his favourite movie role:

"I loved that character. I knew that to play a guy smarter than myself, I'd have to be calm. I think that people who are really smart see everything and therefore they never have those little ups and downs of excitements and lows. So to prepare, I would do yoga. It seemed to help me look cold. It was minimal acting in a kind of way and he got minimal performances out of all of us, which keeps it a nice clean movie to still look at.

"Mike was dealing with such a cold subject full of madness and possession but he seemed to have such a loving mentality and real humanity. He had such a wonderful relationship with the cameraman and all the technicians. I remember that they were so excited to be doing something that had never been done before and being asked to extend themselves. We all couldn't get over how he'd made a Warner Bros' film stage into such an authentic-looking hospital. But Mike had such strong ideas about how the film was supposed to be and how it was to be mounted. He knew roughly what he wanted before he got there and yet, at the same time, he was improvisational with the actors. He always made it feel like a collaboration, which is the easiest kind of atmosphere in which to work. Working on that film was a really pleasurable experience. With Mike, it's all invisible – there's no pain, no strain, no histrionics. Compared with other directors I've worked with, he's top of the list."

Hodges admits to being a big fan of improvisation: "A film is alive. You shouldn't stifle it. You should never over art-direct, over conceive, over research, or walk in with an exact idea of how

"A film is alive. You shouldn't stifle it. You should never over art-direct, over conceive, over research, or walk in with an exact idea of how things should be done." Mike Hodges

things should be done. An actor and a location can always give you something you don't expect. Wonderful accidents happen. You've got to dance with a film, let it live."

With *The Terminal Man*, Hodges has, in fact, made a black-and-white film. His visual style involves having the scenes outside the

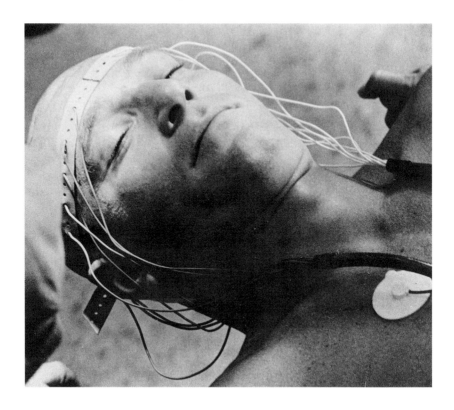

hospital as clinical as the ones inside it. Contrasted with the darkness of Benson's hospital room are the doctors' ultra-clean, futuristic homes, decked out in the same white-on-white colour scheme as the wards they work in. In the hospital, these professionals wear bright white robes and aprons and during out-of-work hours, they dress in black formal dress.

Benson (George Segal) undergoes a computer implantation in The Terminal Man

Hodges' decision to, at one point, use an extract from the old black-and-white movie *Them!* (1955), ties in well with the concept of creating a cold thriller, absent of bright colours, although the idea for the look of the film didn't come from other movies:

"My inspiration came from the American painter Edward Hopper who was relatively unknown in the UK in those days, and up until then, 1974, I'd certainly never heard of him. Something made me pick up this voluminous book of his paintings in Pickwick's bookstore on Hollywood Boulevard. I opened it and

SEND WHEN READY MIND CONTROL 77

there was my film. There was the sheer loneliness of urban America framed on every page. I can remember at that moment deciding to strip my film down to match the loneliness that Hopper had captured. I still have that book."

Hodges ordered in half-a-million dollars worth of surgical and computer hardware for the production, which in the early 1970s was big money. The sophisticated gear included a headless computerized robot, a gleaming X-ray machine and operating table, monitors and gurneys. It was all there to lend authenticity to a brain operation which was carefully researched and plotted by three of Los Angeles' finest brain surgeons.

The actual operation took weeks to film and constituted about a third of the film's playing time. Hodges took great pains to make it as authentic and clinical as he could:

"I didn't want to let the audience off the hook with that particular scene. I wanted them to realize that mind control of this dimension was a reality. I wanted them to see what it is like to put wires into the head of a man. It was very unpleasant for George Segal lying for long periods on the operating table! I really was concerned for him. We devised a way of covering his face during the surgery so that I could use a stand-in, a lie-in to be more accurate. That helped a lot.

"Joan Hackett was very impressive, I think, as Dr Ross. She was perfect for the part. She even cut off her beautiful long hair to make herself appear more like a doctor who has little time for vanity. We looked at hours of surgical films and lectures so that she was fully introduced to the character she played.

"I don't usually storyboard but for the operation sequence I had to. If I hadn't have storyboarded those scenes, I'd have gone crazy trying to remember all of the different shots. It was all in the detail.

"At first, having used only locations on *Get Carter* and *Pulp*, I had to be dragged kicking and screaming into the studio. I was desperate to shoot the operation scene in a real hospital. After looking at every possible operating theatre in Los Angeles, I realized there was nowhere we could do it and have the freedom

necessary. Eventually, my production designer, Fred Hartman convinced me that we should build our own theatre in the studio. Fred did me a big favour. I ended up loving every minute of it! Since then I've always loved shooting in studios. For a filmmaker, it is sheer bliss. Everything is possible and you are in total control of light, sound, everything. In the studio you can be a conjuror. It's like working in a magic box where you can create anything, even the elements – sun, rain, or snow.

"For the first time I started to think of myself of a proper filmmaker. I felt I was making a film in the way my favourite directors did when I was a kid. All those films I'd seen in the late forties and fifties. Back to the very first one I'd ever seen, *Top Hat*, and films like Powell and Pressburger's *The Red Shoes*. And, of

Mike Hodges on the huge Warner Bros. set for The Terminal Man

course, all studio-based musicals, *Singin' in the Rain* and *An American in Paris.* I never missed any of the musicals. Weird, I can't watch any of them now. I don't know why."

Crichton's original novel was stuffed with techno jargon to lend his plot realism. Although Hodges captured his overall idea of mind-control by computer, in the name of medicine, he decided to concentrate more on the human element. The focus is shifted to the anxiety of losing control, something we all share. Benson's wary relationship with computers and machines is something we recognize, even more so now than when *The Terminal Man* was made. Like *Pulp* it is a very prescient film.

Before *The Terminal Man*, in *Pulp* Hodges had satirized Catholicism, with a very funny scene involving a line-up of identical priests (Gilbert's assassin is disguised as a priest). Here, in *The Terminal Man*, Hodges looks more seriously at the religion. He made his hero a Catholic. But when Harry Benson turns to his religion for help, it can't oblige. Nothing and no one can help Benson. He has his third attack and, out of control, strangles the priest. In Crichton's book, the climax is a shoot-out in the basement of the hospital. In Hodges' film, it takes place in a cemetery. He felt that the film couldn't *just* be about the perversion of scientific progress or science replacing religion. Instead, it had to deal with the harsh realities of life and death:

"I can understand why Crichton wanted to end the film with a shoot-out in the hospital basement. It's a technological end to a technological problem. That's perfectly valid but, for me, that's unsatisfactory! It doesn't go deep enough. So, even though Crichton didn't agree with me, I changed the ending, and with it the whole mood of the film.

"Technology isn't just out there on its own. We create it and we use it. Ultimately, it has to relate to humans. When it doesn't, when it de-humanizes, there is a problem. I felt that the breaking in, the opening up of a person's brain to change its circuitry is like invading a foreign country, or opening a tomb. Change it and we are somebody else. Of course, some of our relatives shrank the heads of their enemy and wore them. In the British Museum the

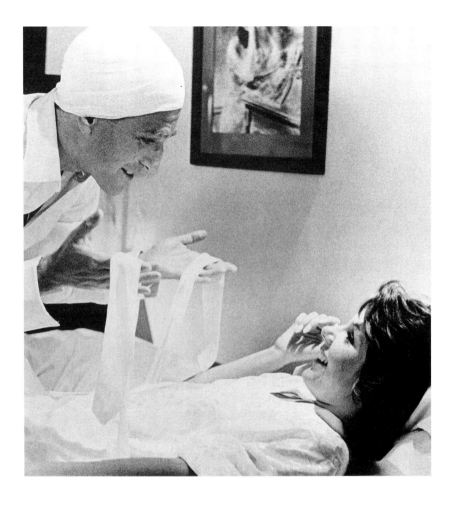

other day I came across a skull turned into the bell of a trumpet.
Blowing a tune through an enemy's head is rather touching, I think.
In short the head has always been considered somewhere special.
Maybe some think it's where the soul resides? If it is, opening it up
is like opening up the tabernacle in a church.

Back with his girl
Angela Black (Jill
Clayburgh) before
another seizure
takes hold

"It's a film about the inevitably impersonal coldness of any
institution, and hospitals in particular. Apart from Dr Ross, and
obviously Harry, the rest of them are cold and detached. It's a
curious film and is divided into two distinctive parts. The first part
is about the operation. The second is a more conventional thriller

with a series of deaths and the culmination of the whole piece. Welding the two was not easy but the visual style hopefully helped."

Later, in an HBO television drama *W.G.O.D* (1985) and in *A Prayer for the Dying* (1987), Hodges would also turn what could have been run-of-the-mill thrillers into quite complex, serious films, brimming with his own quirky references and general distrust of religions, especially Catholicism. Hodges has only one regret about *The Terminal Man:*

"I agreed to a change early in the film which I regret deeply. Feedback from the studio concluded that audiences had no one to root for. This was incomprehensible to me – if they can't root for Harry Benson, who the hell are they going to root for? The guy was completely trapped with nowhere to go, no one to turn to, but they couldn't root for him because he wasn't coated in sugar. Harry wasn't very affable. The studio suggested I switch a restaurant scene where the hospital PR man is briefing the surgeons on the media coverage. If placed close to the beginning, before the opening credit sequence, we could insert before-and-after photographs of Harry and his family in happier times before the car accident, Harry's battered wife, Harry under police escort, and so on. This was meant to make him more sympathetic. In my view it didn't make a scrap of difference. The scene is absolutely unnecessary and I've been trying ever since to get it removed if only from the DVD. I've failed because nobody gives a sod except me. I could kick myself for agreeing to it in the first place."

Before the scene in the restaurant, however, there is the prison sequence in which an anonymous eye peers through a security peephole. It's a guard staring into Benson's cell.

He asks his colleague: "What's wrong with him?"

"He's bananas," is the reply.

This is also the point when Glenn Gould's piano begins a Goldberg Variation, enhancing the film's eerie beginning. A similar sequence comes at the end, with the comment: "They want you next". A shot of the same eye staring through the peephole brings this mesmerizing film to a close.

TERRY MALICK

8 July

Dear Mr. Hodges,

I have just come from seeing "The
Terminal Man" and want you to know what a
magnificent, overwhelming picture it is. You
achieve moods that I've never experienced in
the movies before, though it's only in hope
of finding them that I keep going. Your
images make me understand what an image is,
not a pretty picture but something that should
pierce one through like an arrow and speak
in a language all its own. Which is perhaps
why I cannot say just what it meant to see
George Segal stumbling into the mausoleum at
Forest Lawn or crushing the rose in his hands.
Still, even if I can't, I felt in those moment
(and countless others) that I knew just what
sadness is, and just how one's life can slip
away or go bad, and just what it's like to be
here, unrequired, on this earth. I'm running
on, I guess, but don't let that diminish my
credibility. You must understand what a rare,
extraordinary thing you've done, after all.
My wife, reading over my shoulder, echoes
all these feelings.

Sincerely,

In the end, *The Terminal Man* wasn't even given a release in the UK and, in the US, after bad previews and terrible reviews, it was dumped.

"I think American audiences found the film too uncompromising, too tough to take, and perhaps they had a problem accepting George Segal in a serious role for a change. At the time, he'd developed a reputation as a light comic actor, but I decided on him for the film mainly because, wait for it, I thought the audience would root for him. I still think he is terribly good in it. He's a very good actor.

"While waiting for my first preview in LA my wife and I went to see a preview of Terrence Malick's first film, *Badlands* (1974). It was also with Warner Bros. We both loved it but the rest of the audience didn't seem to enjoy it. Again it was too tough for them. It was then I realized it would be the same fate for *The Terminal Man*. I remember turning to Jean in the cinema and saying that I thought I'd made it too spare, too close to the bone. I meant to write to Terrence Malick to congratulate him but I didn't for whatever reason.

"I really felt bad about this when, out of the blue, I received a letter headed 'Terry Malick' but with no address. It was the most wonderful letter to get when I was feeling so bruised by the negative reaction to the *The Terminal Man*. I replied, of course, but because I had no address I sent it care of Warner Bros. Months later I received the letter back stamped 'Not known at this address'. So the man who had made one of the great films of the decade was not known by the studio that had financed it. Perfect.

When I eventually managed to contact Terrence I sent him the returned letter with a note: 'That's showbusiness!'

During pre-production, Hodges received a letter from Michael Crichton, who clearly didn't like Hodges' script. Since then, it looks like the man behind *Jurassic Park* and *ER* has changed his mind. As George Segal recalls: "At the time, I remember Michael Crichton was feeling usurped because he'd just decided he wanted to start directing but I guess had already sold the film rights to *The Terminal Man*. But since that time, while critics began reappraising the film, he sent me a note extolling the film. So it looks like he came round too!"

Now, it seems, viewers and critics are re-evaluating this underrated film. When it plays on television, reviews in the film guides are a lot kinder. In fact, *The Terminal Man* is a film that plays on television regularly in America, where it was first rejected. Hodges says he knows this to be the case because of the large residuals he receives from US television networks.

That a film has found a substantial audience two decades after it was made could mean that people's taste in movies has changed, although it does seem to suggest that if the studio had bothered to get behind *The Terminal Man* in the first place, it would have met with more success. It's also a good reason for Warner Bros. to release this lost gem on DVD.

Back Home: Screenplays

Chapter 5

"All directors go out of fashion. Even Bergman,
even Fellini. That's just the way it is."
Mike Hodges

After finishing The Terminal Man Mike Hodges returned home. It soon became apparent the film was a disaster both critically and at the box office. He decided to write another original script. The idea had come to him while in LA.

He'd come across a book called The Pit, a documentary account of a self-improvement course run by Holiday Magic, a company that sold cosmetics to the public at a discount for them to retail at a higher price. The follow-up was a weekend course on "leadership dynamics" for those who hadn't shifted their product. The book was about one course that had gone badly wrong.

"This happened before all those trendy mind-expanding courses, like EST, started up. This was grass roots stuff, innocents who could ill-afford the $1,000 fee. The book described how these people had checked in to a Holiday Inn, then were taken to a conference room with blacked-out windows, one room for the men, another for the women. In each there was a hangman's rope dangling from the ceiling, a coffin, a full-sized cross and a cage – props to be used for psychological inspiration. They weren't allowed to speak to each other, smoke or make telephone calls. If any of them saw another breaking these rules they had to report them to the instructors. From the Friday night until the Sunday night, the instructors would keep these men and women without sleep and would constantly interrogate them. If they decided a person wasn't motivated, 'dead', they'd put them into the coffin and make others sit on top of it for hours. When they were eventually let out the victim would feel, not surprisingly, 'alive'. Those overweight they'd put naked in the cage and pour hotel swill over them. If they decided someone was a masochist, they would hang them from the cross.

"The whole process was meant to turn these innocents into achievers. The instructors would whip the class into a frenzy, berating them about their status in life, the money they earned, the cars they drove, the realty they owned, and so on. It was the perfect metaphor for the American dream turned into a nightmare. And this particular weekend the course turned violent, more violent than usual that is.

"I was still at Warner Bros., so I suggested to reconstruct what happened with actors, over two weekends, for free. But the executive who read the book absolutely hated it. He was horrified! But not horrified in the way I was. He was horrified that anyone would want to film such a disgusting, even sacrilegious, event highlighting the excesses of the capitalist way of life.

"Back in England, a friend of mine told me that the same course had actually occurred in a hotel in London in 1974. This time a reporter had infiltrated the course and blew the whistle on it. The organizers vanished back to America. I had never thought of it happening here. It was then I decided to write a script called *Mid-Atlantic*. It's about a seedy public relations man scraping a living in an out-of-season seaside resort. In those days hardly anyone here had been to America, and that was his dream. America as 'the promised land'; that's what I wanted to write about. My hero, Mark Miles, was ready to go; he even had a mid-Atlantic accent. He gets a call from an old friend who wants him to negotiate a deal with a hotel for this American course that's coming into town. I had picked up where the actual story ended. The Americans had vanished from London – only to turn up at the seaside. And my hero was about to have an object

Previous page and below: Hodges talks about his career at the American Cinematheque's retrospective in 1998

lesson in the realities of American culture. It was a black comedy. What else could it be."

Malcolm McDowell was going to play Mark Miles, and Jack Nicholson, then in the UK making *The Shining*, was interested in playing the course guru, Hermann Temple. But after four years of trying to obtain funding, Hodges gave up. Several times over the next decade interest was shown in the project but it never went into production. In time, everything Hodges was fearful of happening in his homeland happened:

"In 1979 Thatcher came to power and that was it! If you read my script today, you wouldn't believe how quaint it is. No need to shoot the film now. We've done it for real. We've become a tacky theme park for rip-off capitalism. When *Mid-Atlantic* was being conceived nobody in this country talked about money. The subject was considered beyond the pale. Now, it's the major topic of conversation. There were no money programmes on television and radio. The FT and DOW index wasn't on the News. When I first went to America I couldn't believe the national obsession with money. Friendly eyes would literally change, become steely, when the dollar sign rang up. And I thought it would never happen here. How wrong can you be?"

During the four-year period Hodges was trying to get funding, he also wrote two other screenplays. The first was called *The Chilean Club* (1976), to be produced by Michael Klinger, and the second was a vehicle for Donald Sutherland called *Spare Parts* (1977). Neither of them attracted backing.

Then Hodges made what he says was "a gross error". In 1976, he had been asked to direct the feature *The Omen* (1976), but had turned it down, finding the script, "laughable … completely silly". The film was directed by Richard Donner and grossed millions at the box office.

With one doomed project after another, Hodges became increasingly worried about the state of his career.

"Although I'd had a good start to my career, making three interesting films by 1974, it was now 1978 and I hadn't made a movie for four years – so I thought I'd better quickly do another one!"

Despite turning down the original, the producers of *The Omen* came back to Hodges with a treatment for a sequel. It describes how, seven years after killing his parents (Gregory Peck and Lee Remick), Damien has been adopted by his aunt and billionaire uncle (Lee Grant and William Holden). But, even with a new family, the omens surrounding Damien's true heritage won't let go. The sequel would show Damien discovering who he really is and what he was destined to do. He, Satan, would inherit the world.

Hodges loved the synopsis.

"Politically, it was right up my street. Damien's uncle controls a vast complex of international corporations. Beelzebub's acolytes are already in position, holding various administrative positions, waiting for Damien to arrive.

"So we're back to one of my favourite subjects, corporate power. And what is this particular network of corporations interested in? Cornering the world's food markets and introducing genetically modified food. That was in 1978, long before Monsanto was on every environmentalist's lips.

"I couldn't believe the irony of being sent this treatment. Here I was being offered an unwittingly anti-capitalist film by a film conglomerate, Twentieth Century Fox, about an even bigger conglomerate run by the Devil. It was bizarre."

Hodges soon found himself in Chicago directing *Damien: Omen II*. After three weeks' shooting, however, he walked:

> "It was really my own fault. They wanted a horror movie and that was the part that didn't interest me. So when they hauled me in to say we were going too slow, I bowed out gracefully and gratefully. I said I would stay until they found another director. I needn't have bothered as they already had a replacement."
>
> Mike Hodges

"It was *my* Hollywood nightmare! It was like a Terry Southern novella. Have you ever read *The Magic Christian?* He also wrote the screenplay for *Dr Strangelove*. First of all, there were these horror stories circulating about what happened to people who worked on *Omen I*. Everything from fatal car crashes to an accidental beheading like in the

film. As if this wasn't enough the guy who had the original idea for the series, needless to say a born again Christian, came into my office and told me the Devil would try everything to stop me making the film. It was crazy, idiotic, but it was also very weird and unsettling.

"It soon became obvious that I was shooting a film different from the one they wanted. I wanted to show wealth as size like Welles had done in *Citizen Kane*. This meant that the lighting took time and we got behind schedule. Initially they were after the cameraman but I wouldn't have that so the big guns turned on me.

"It was really my own fault. They wanted a horror movie and that was the part that didn't interest me. So when they hauled me in to say we were going too slow, I bowed out gracefully and gratefully. I said I would stay until they found another director. I needn't have bothered as they already had a replacement."

Don Taylor took over as director, although it's not too difficult to spot the scenes Hodges directed. These scenes, in particular those filmed in the food laboratories and the military academy, are far more subtle than the rest, which follow the familiar *Omen* pattern of grisly murders and shock value.

"I have to say, though, that Richard Donner did a great job on *Omen I* with unpromising material," says Hodges. "And the great thing for me, the only redeemable feature, was getting to work with William Holden.

Director Abe Polonsky (left) and film marketer Mike Kaplan (right) greet Mike Hodges at the American Cinematheque's retrospective in Los Angeles

It took me back to the cinemas in Salisbury where I'd first seen him, usually in Billy Wilder films. I loved Holden. He rang me up on my last night in Chicago and said he hoped we'd work together again – but on something less violent. We never did, sadly."

As part of Fox's commercial horror franchise, *Damien: Omen II* went on to box office success. Once again Hodges returned to England.

After leaving *Damien: Omen II*, Hodges worked on another original screenplay, *Blood and Thunder* (1978), this one to star Vanessa Redgrave and Jane Fonda, who, following the success of their movie *Julia* (1977), both wanted to co-star in another film together. The project failed to attract industry interest.

Another original screenplay Hodges wrote during this period, *Say Goodnight, Lilian – Goodnight* (1978), was based on his observation of LA's comedy clubs:

"Living in Los Angeles in the mid-seventies, I became obsessed by stand-up comics and used to go to the Comedy Store on Sunset Boulevard three or four times a week. I didn't care who was on; I just wanted to witness raw chutzpah. Every night I marvelled at these driven people. It was like bull fighting, the supposed comedians would charge on stage, horns down!

"The obsession had to surface somewhere and it did in *Say Goodnight, Lilian – Goodnight*. It starts with this patently wealthy woman leaving her palatial home, and checking into a sleazy hotel. There she changes her appearance with a blonde wig, an overtly sexy outfit and loads of make-up: we immediately think she's a hooker. Instead she steps on stage at a strip club; she's the comic working between the acts. Her patter is a vitriolic diatribe about an imaginary husband. The husband, of course, isn't imaginary, and the act is based on her unhappy marriage. A gossip columnist gets wind of this and exposes the deception. The millionaire businessman husband becomes a laughing stock.

"They split and the husband becomes a recluse. We watch their roles reverse. She becomes a major national comedy star, a bit like Joan Rivers, performing in Las Vegas, while her husband is bankrupted. It has a bittersweet ending. She's driven crazy with fame but goes under fighting. Her final target is the desperation behind celebrity mania.

"It was a great role for an actress. Among others I tried Carol

Burnett, who I thought would have been brilliant, and none of them were interested.

"At one point, the producers thought the problem was with her comedy routine. They brought in some guy who wrote material for Bette Middler. It was a dumb thing to do. How could you treat her act

> "Hollywood actresses . . . say they can't find good women's roles. Well, I have written a lot of good female parts and found that when it comes to the nitty gritty, if the material is too strong, they just don't want to know. Image is more important." Mike Hodges

as something separate: I mean, the comedy act *was* her life. Of course, they completely fucked up the whole thing, leaving another of my projects in tatters.

"It did the rounds of all the major studios. Curiously, some years later a film called *Punchline* (1988) with Sally Field and Tom Hanks, was released. There were striking similarities.

"I'm still proud of the *Say Goodnight, Lilian – Goodnight* screenplay. It's amused me watching the vacuous celebrity game grow like a strange weed entangling us all. Now, even the broadsheets carry news about idiot celebrities. Again this was a script based on my observations of America. What happens there is seemingly bound to happen everywhere, unfortunately. As a culture America is very contagious.

"Hollywood actresses, in particular, say they can't find good women's roles. Well, I have written a lot of good female parts and found that when it comes to the nitty gritty, if the material is too strong, they just don't want to know. Image is more important. I found this with *Black Rainbow*, with *Say Goodnight, Lilian – Goodnight*, with *Blood and Thunder*, and other films. I'm sad about that."

Understandably disheartened, Hodges began to wonder if his cinema career was over. Although he returned from the US once again, to write scripts from his base in England, none of them were attracting finance.

But then his luck changed. In the spring of 1979, came the call from one of Hollywood's most powerful movie producers . . .

Disco in the Sky: Flash Gordon

"This was the first $27 million movie ever improvised!"
Mike Hodges

Pulp had scored with the critics but failed commercially; *The Terminal Man* was a disaster, critically and at the box office; and to most people it looked like Hodges had been fired from *Damien: Omen II*, even though his departure was, in fact, an amicable arrangement. All in all, it looked like his career was in very bad shape.

Flash Gordon, a movie update of the 1930s' comic strip, was the film that put him back on the rails.

Out of the blue, Hodges received a call from his filmmaker friend Nic Roeg, who was originally lined up to direct the movie.

"Nic called to say that Dino de Laurentiis was anxious to meet me, and could I come to the Connaught Hotel. When I got there, Dino took me to one side and explained that they were looking for a director to do *Flash Gordon 2*. Nic was doing the original but they wanted to capitalize on the expensive sets being built and shoot the sequel back to back. He asked if I would write and direct it. I turned it down. I'd just had a bad experience doing the *Omen* sequel, and wasn't interested in doing sequels anyway.

"Not long after this meeting Dino and Nic fell out. Nic left the film, and for reasons known only to him, Dino came back to me. This time it was to do the original *Flash Gordon*. I still resisted. I didn't know anything about *Flash Gordon,* or about making a special effects movie. It was a big project and I really had no idea how to go about it. In the end, it was my kids who got me to say 'yes'! Dino immediately flew me out to New York on Concorde.

"The plane was full of businessmen, all with briefcases. They were all poring over important-looking documents and computer read-outs while I was clutching my bumper volume of *Flash Gordon*! The other passengers looked at me like I was retarded.

"The first person I met was Danilo Donato, Dino's Italian production designer. Danilo had designed many of Federico Fellini films, including my favourite, *Casanova* (1976). The only problem was that he spoke no English at all!

"Donato had already completed drawings of the planets Mongo and Arboria and Frigia. He had two minions unroll them and that completely freaked me. They must have been about 10 feet high by 20 feet wide. Dino's office was high up in a skyscraper overlooking

Previous page:
Sam J Jones as
Flash Gordon, foot-
ball quarterback
and saviour of the
universe!

Central Park, and when they held them up, these drawings literally blocked out the light. It was crazy and left me even more daunted by the prospect of doing the film. But by then, I had already accepted."

The original script, written by Michael Allin, was soon abandoned. Another was written by Lorenzo Semple Jr, the creator of the 1960s' television series *Batman*. Semple, with encouragement from Hodges, went back to the original source material, the strip cartoon. The only concession to the contemporary was making Flash a quarterback with the New York Jets.

Semple had Flash Gordon, beautiful reporter Dale Arden and eminent scientist Alexis Zarkov getting sucked through a black hole into the pantomime galaxy of Mongo, from which Ming the Merciless is trying to destroy the world. And of course, only a football star can save the universe from destruction.

"Disco in the sky"
Pauline Kael on *Flash Gordon*

Hodges worked with Semple on the revised screenplay and then began shooting some of the model work.

"After I shot some of this early model material, I found out that Dino had looked at the rushes without me being present – which is a cardinal sin. A producer never looks at rushes without the director being present. If I'm honest I think I'd realized I was completely out of my depth and wanted out. So, using his breach of the rules, I told him I was quitting. I heard later, from other sources, that he immediately told his line producer to bring in his list of directors. It was bizarre because he'd kept calling me Nic ever since we'd started. Now I knew why! When he looked down this list, he pointed to a name and said 'get me that one'. Well the name he'd pointed to was 'Mike Hodges'. Now the line producer had to tell him this was the director who'd just left! That was Dino for you.

"But, needless to say, Dino and I made it up. We agreed that if he had any grievances he was to talk to me in private and not in front of the crew. And he certainly wasn't to look at rushes without me being present. We didn't have any further bust-ups. I even grew to love the monster."

It was difficult casting Flash, according to Hodges:

"The character of Flash is really as thick as a plank. There's an innocence about him that's difficult to find these days. All the people we saw – all these name stars – were not right, physically or otherwise. I suppose they were too knowing.

"I remember Kurt Russell was a contender and he did a camera test. He wasn't right, though – well, I didn't think so at the time. Dennis Hopper was considered for Zarkov, which also didn't materialize. But Topol was perfect casting for that role. Anyway, Dino's mother-in-law, Silvana Mangano's mother if you will, spotted Sam J Jones on the television game show *Hollywood Squares*. She suggested him. Sam was working for Blake Edwards in Hawaii on the film *10* (1978). We got him in for a screen test, dyed his hair blond, and that was it. End of search. He got the part."

With Sam J Jones as Flash, Hodges' next task was to cast the female reporter Dale Arden:

"We also had problems casting the Dale Arden part. A Canadian actress was chosen. She was good but the deal fell through – mainly because Dino had decided she was too thin! At first he thought pasta would do the trick but then decided she didn't have enough fun about her. Dino's thinking process is very distinctive.

"As it happened our first casting trawl included Melody Anderson and she'd already done a camera test for us. So we switched to her, and I'm pleased we did. She did a fantastic job and looked very like Dale in the original strip.

"Next in line was Ming the Merciless. Max Von Sydow was a friend of Dino's and agreed to play Ming. I'd only seen him in Ingmar Bergman's films. My God, I'd get to chew the fat with Death from *The Seventh Seal*. Another casting coup was Timothy Dalton as Prince Barin. Tim with his moustache looked amazing – just like Errol Flynn. Back then, before he got to play James Bond, I think I'm right in saying he was mainly employed as a character actor. I remember him being terrific as Colonel Christie in *Agatha* (1979). As I watched

I couldn't work out why he hadn't already become a big star. He really did have the quality of Flynn.

Prince Barin   "I was also pleased when John Osborne agreed to play a small

(Timothy Dalton)   role. If you look carefully you'll see he's the high priest in Arboria.

rules the jungle   He's the one banging his staff up and down and looks like he's

kingdom of Arboria   masturbating. We'd become good friends since *Get Carter*. John was

always happy to escape writing chores. There's a lot of hanging around in filming and he was always wicked company."

Shooting *Flash Gordon* took 10 months to complete. Hodges found the process both amusing and bizarre:

"It was like surfing. From the casting, through the filming, in and out of the editing rooms and around the dubbing theatre, the ride was completely manic and totally improvised. Every day I and crew, especially my operator, Gordon Haymen, were dancing on our feet, making it up as we went along. It was great.

"I honestly thought the film would never see the light of a projector because it was so chaotic. One day, in the middle of the madness, I turned to Dino and asked him why he'd chosen me to direct the movie. I'd assumed he'd say it was because of *Get Carter* or *The Terminal Man*; instead he just said: 'I a-like-a-your-a face!' Here I was directing this blockbuster because the producer liked my face! Dino's primitive belief in the phizog revealing all didn't stop with me! During casting, if I met someone promising, my secretary would alert his secretary at the other end of the corridor. He would come to my office, take one look at the actor in question, nod or shake his head, grunt and walk off! It always made me laugh but was disconcerting for the actors.

"It didn't help that my Italian was non-existent; on a par with Danilo's English. And the same applied to most of his design team! There was this huge team of Italian artisans housed around Shepperton studios. They were talented, warm and smiling, brilliant in everything except English. I just had to relax and let it all happen. Once I did that, every day was like Christmas.

"Danilo, although creating some amazing costumes, wasn't the most pragmatic designer. I don't think he ever read the script so he never knew the functional aspects of the costumes or sets. I remember the 'pig men' coming into Ming's palace for the first time. They had to be led on the set like blind people. They had no way of seeing through Danilo's costumes! It was so weird watching them bumbling around, bumping into each other, trying to work out where the hell they were, that I made them sightless in the film! But then I used everything that happened to our advantage.

"There was another scene where Dale had to beat up several 'pig men' with karate chops followed by a somersault. She arrived on set in a metal dress that weighed a ton *and* she was wearing high heels! The poor girl could hardly walk. It looked great but was completely impractical. So I had her take the high heels off, put them down like outside a hotel door, beat up a 'pig man', move the shoes, beat up another 'pig man', do the somersault, pick up the shoes and exit. I turned what potentially was a disaster into a whole new comedy sequence with the damn shoes! It wasn't in the script, of course. Stuff like this would be a daily occurrence.

"At one point I really had to put my foot down with Danilo. Many people say how camp *Flash Gordon* is and, although I can see what they mean, I really didn't intend for the character of Flash to be camp or gay in any way. But Danilo, who was gay, had designed this diamante T-shirt for Flash to wear. It was this tank top with a plunging neckline! That's when I put my foot down.

"In the end, I had no alternative but to improvize. There was no way I could control it. Until *Flash Gordon* I'd always managed to keep a tight rein on all my films, but not this one. It must be the most expensive film improvized ever! I made myself relax with it. I'd turn up, look at the set and the costumes and make use of whatever was there. It was a great learning curve for me. And this relaxed atmosphere extended to the script. Again we would adapt it to the circumstances, changing or adding dialogue as we went along."

And some of those dialogue exchanges were extremely funny.

Flash and Dale are reunited on the Hawkmen's City in the Sky.

Dale: "Oh Flash, I've got so much to tell you."

Flash: "Save it for our children."

And in another scene.

Dale (as she's pulled away from all the fighting): "Please. Can't you see I've just got engaged?"

And how about the scene in the dungeon where Prince Barin and Zarkov are chained to a wall together.

Prince Barin: "Tell me more about this man Houdini?"

"Dino took it all so seriously, and I could never quite get to grips with that. He once said to me, 'Remember, Michael, Flash-a-de-

Gordon, he save-a de world!' He really did think we were making a serious film and kept asking why the crew laughed every morning when we watched the rushes. So I had to ask them *not* to laugh! What else are you meant to do but laugh at a comic strip? When Alex Raymond had first created the strip in the 1930s man was a long way from landing on the moon. But by 1980 we'd been there, done that! So here we have in our film Zarkov building his space rocket in a conservatory! It *had* to be tongue-in-cheek."

Principal photography ended after 17 weeks and the crew broke for Christmas. Around this time there was a fall-out between Dino de Laurentiis and Sam J Jones's management, and Hodges was told that his star wasn't coming back. This meant he had to employ a stunt double in second unit shots including Flash on the space bike. He also had to find someone to impersonate Jones for those lines that had to be re-voiced.

Because Jones had departed, it also meant Dino de Laurentiis and Universal studios were left without the star to publicize the picture.

Above: Flash in chains with Major Kala (Marrangelo Melato)

Previous page: Disco in the Sky: Brian Blessed as Prince Vultan with Flash, flying to the rescue

Instead they tried to build the campaign around Max Von Sydow as Ming: "which is ridiculous. You can't have a film called *Flash Gordon* with posters that major on Ming. It was a great shame because Sam worked hard on the film, and had a nice personality. He *was* Flash, the all-American boy. He would have gone down a storm on all the chat shows there." Continues Hodges:

"Nevertheless, throughout all of this chaos, I had the best time of my life. It was absolutely wonderful. It was like cooking a soufflé. Whenever I watch it, I recall the fun we all had doing it – and you can see that sense of fun up there on the screen. It was hard work and a long process but worth it. It did well at the box office and people around the world love it. I often meet fans who know every line. Unfortunately some of those lines are embarrassing."

Critics, however, have been blunt about the film's flaws. Many criticized the special effects which were admittedly primitive compared to today's standards. "We had no computer imagery whatsoever," says Hodges. "It was all done against blue backgrounds and then superimposed. Although we tried to make it look moderately real I never wanted it to look slick. With a film like *Flash Gordon*, that would have been disastrous because it wasn't a realistic film to begin with!"

George Lucas had originally wanted to make *Flash Gordon* but when he couldn't obtain the rights he made *Star Wars* (1977) instead. There's no doubt that elements from Alex Raymond's comic strip feature prominently in both *Star Wars* and *The Empire Strikes Back* (1980).

"George Lucas had originally wanted to make *Flash Gordon* but when he couldn't obtain the rights he made *Star Wars* (1977) instead." Mike Hodges

Perhaps if Lucas had got his hands on *Flash Gordon*, he'd have turned it into one of his usual strait-laced affairs. Mark Hammill as Flash, Harrison Ford as Barin, Alec Guinness as Dr Zarkov, Peter Cushing as Ming and Carrie Fisher as Princess Aura … And still Lucas makes out that *Star Wars* is an original story.

Hodges' film is the perfect antidote to formulaic sci-fi epics, an alternative to the Lucas–Spielberg approach. Shamelessly entertaining, *Flash Gordon* is sexy, lavish, wild and absurd – and comes with a perfect pounding rock soundtrack by Queen.

While films such as *Superman – the Movie* (1977) tried to distance themselves from their original source material, Hodges and his team embraced it and recreated the visual atmosphere of Raymond's comic strips. Years later, capturing the visual style of original comic book material would come into vogue again with *Batman, Dick Tracey* and *The Shadow* to name but a few. *Flash* was there first!

In the end Mike Hodges' *Flash Gordon* can be watched at various levels. At one level, it's a non-stop adventure for the kids. On another, there is hidden sexual innuendo and jokes for the adults. Hodges undoubtedly did a great job of treading a fine line between sexy tongue-in-cheek laughs and Saturday morning cinema.

The psychedelic art-deco sets make up for any glitches in the effects and the general sense of fun makes up for the odd spot of wooden acting! It's easy to see how much Hodges loved making this film and how it helped make up for his previous Hollywood nightmares. And of course, bearing in mind his views on Uncle Sam's foreign policies, it must have been quite rewarding to be able to portray this hero as such a stupid oaf!

Back to the Box and on to Fellini

"Cinema sights have been lowered. The attention span of the younger audience is pretty limited."
Mike Hodges

Not long after the release of *Flash Gordon*, Hodges and his wife, Jean, separated. They divorced in 1982.

"It was a bumpy marriage, for all of its 18 years, and we'd just had enough," says Hodges.

Another work offer was already on the table. This was to write and direct a television thriller for CBS in America. Originally titled *A Private Investigation*, which later became *Missing Pieces,* the producers wanted him to adapt Karl Alexander's novel for their contract star, Elizabeth Montgomery.

Impressed by the novel and desperate to get away from England and the "painful" break-up with his wife, Hodges took the job, despite it meaning a return to LA.

"Los Angeles is not my favourite city. How could it be? Unless of course you like studying the interior décor of your limo! But this time around I had decided to go native, assimilate myself into the place. Among the chosen activities I took up was learning the clarinet, a small light instrument that an itinerant film director – that's how my future appeared then – could take with him anywhere.

"Now, painting has become the greatest joy in my life. And when the work's completed nobody will want to change it." Mike Hodges

"The teacher I ended up with was a rather frail old Jewish jazzer, Gerry. After I'd been blowing away for some months I asked him about the drawings and watercolours taped to the wall of his rundown apartment. I really liked them. It turned out he'd done them himself. So I asked him if he would teach me how to draw, as well as play the clarinet.

"I bought a pad and some charcoals and we began to alternate lessons. Gerry freed me. I hadn't drawn since I was 7, or earlier. He didn't teach me; he just freed me. Of course, because I'd got divorced, it meant that I could now shed all the heavy material stuff – houses and cars and other shit that we'd accumulated as a family.

"It was a weird period of my life, during the making of *Missing Pieces*, sorting out my life and re-evaluating my existence. Now, painting has

Previous page: One of Hodges' paintings, an interest he began in 1982

become the greatest joy in my life. But, of course, unlike filmmaking, it costs next to zilch. And when the work's completed nobody will want to change it.

"I'm eternally grateful to Gerry. We lost touch when I came back home. Sometimes I wonder how he's doing. He was quite ill I think; maybe he's dead. I invited him to the crew showing of *Missing Pieces*. The only music – if you could ever call it that – was a clarinet blowing the scales, badly. It was me. Gerry was mortified, and I mean mortified. You must understand that my early cultural education was nil. NIL! So the process of happening upon every art form has sustained me – and still does – in my adult life. When I got back to the UK, I suddenly locked into contemporary dance. What a revelation that was! My first calling place in any town or city is the art gallery."

Missing Pieces (1982), which eventually aired in the US in May 1983, is an oddly structured film – an engaging role reversal detective mystery in which *Bewitched* star Elizabeth Montgomery turns private eye to track down the killers of her reporter husband, Andy (David Haskell). As Sara Scott, Montgomery is propelled into a case that eventually leads her to the truth about his demise. As so often with Hodges the trail leads to corrupt politicians.

Hodges combines a surrealistic directorial approach, full of flashbacks, with an intriguing stream-of-consciousness narrative thread, as supplied by the main character, Sara Scott. This convention is perfectly executed, establishing a nightmarish momentum that keeps up the curiosity and bolsters the mystery.

It's the third time Hodges' employed the voice-over technique in a film (first *Rumour*, second *Pulp*) and, although not quite as effective as Caine's voice-over narration in *Pulp,* Montgomery manages to pull it off, echoing the detective movies of the 1940s and 1950s. Ron Karabatos nearly steals the film from her, though, as Claude Papzian, the world-weary detective she goes to work for. Louanne is also impressive as Valerie, Montgomery's moody daughter.

Looking at the project now, Hodges comments: "It was an interesting piece I think. I liked the book and the arena in which it takes place – but it really was just a job to keep me busy through my divorce. All divorces are distressing; mine was no exception. At the time I thought it best for all concerned to get out of the way for a while."

On returning to the UK, after this "pleasant interlude", Hodges came down with what he thought was just a bad dose of flu. In fact, he was seriously ill with diverticulitus; a tumour had developed on his lower intestine. He was rushed into hospital to undergo major surgery. "It could have been malignant," explains Hodges, "but that wasn't the case. While I'm philosophical about dying, I certainly had the feeling I might be near the end. Luckily I wasn't."

When Hodges came out of hospital, the chance came to work with one of his cinema heroes, Federico Fellini. His role would be to direct dubbing of the English language version of *And the Ship Sails On (E La Nave Va)* (1983). The offer came from Fellini via Stanley Kubrick:

"Fellini had called Kubrick complaining that he always had an awful time trying to dub his films successfully into English and asked his advice. Stanley said that what he did was to get a known director in each country to dub his films there. It is very smart thinking. That way you get the care and sensitivity of a good director working in his native language. He recommended this approach to Fellini, who then asked who to get in England.

"I knew that Stanley had always been interested in my films. Over the years, I'd heard from various sources that he'd liked *The Terminal Man,* and before that he'd remarked to Malcolm McDowell when they were making *A Clockwork Orange* that he'd liked my television film *Rumour.*"

Still in bad shape from the surgery, Hodges needed work. This job was perfect. He could do it sitting down and have a master lesson in filmmaking at the same time:

"I was very weak but I had to take the job if only to meet Fellini! Since most of the original actors were English, it was pretty straightforward. It wasn't as much of a strain as I'd thought. It was a very gentle, loving film about the world of Italian opera; perfect for someone recuperating from an illness!

"I went to Rome to meet Fellini and watch the film with him. They had a guide track, albeit a terrible one. Of course I had to watch each scene time and time again. But it wasn't at all boring. It was the opposite, fascinating – seeing how Fellini worked. I learnt so much from that exercise."

Federico Fellini's film is one of the late master's most fanciful projects, while simultaneously striking one of the most sombre notes in the director's filmography.

It's July 1914, the eve of World War I and the coming destruction of Europe's old, cultured aristocracy. A luxury liner leaves Italy with the

> "... seeing how Fellini worked. I learnt so much from that exercise."
> Mike Hodges

ashes of the famous opera singer Tetua. The boat is filled with her friends, opera singers, actors and all kinds of exotic people – even a rhinoceros! The point of the voyage is to scatter the ashes of this world-famous diva.

During the funeral voyage, the captain saves a party of Serbian refugees, refugees who had escaped the first tremors of the War, from drowning. Fellini uses the entrance of these refugees, and their confrontations with the rich passengers, to comment on the unreality of their privileged lives. The blatantly unrealistic studio set, with a painted sky, paper moon and cellophane sea, serves to emphasize the artificiality of their world.

Fellini orchestrates the piece as pure artifice, outside real time and space. The stylistic storytelling is wonderfully offbeat and visually captivating. And the strange collection of characters, plot twist and diversions, and general quirkiness of this film is so oddly compelling, you can't help but be totally caught up in it. The stupendous finale is enough to make the film worthwhile if nothing else.

The time spent on the Fellini film paid off for Hodges on his next project. "Working with Danilo Donati on *Flash Gordon* meant that I looked at a lot of his work with Fellini," he says. "I loved the theatricality of it and had him illustrate how they had created so many wonderful visual effects. This, coupled with my recent exposure to Fellini himself, influenced me in my approach to another television project the following year."

Within hours of the announcement of the Nobel Peace Prize being awarded to the Catholic leader of Solidarity, Lech Walesa, it so happened that filming began on *Squaring the Circle* (1984). This gripping two-hour TV drama was written by Tom Stoppard and based on the struggles of Walesa, who, with his union of unarmed workers, defied the might of the Russian empire in 16 historic months that shook the totalitarian world.

Hodges was approached to direct the piece. He was about the eighth director to be asked.

"Stoppard's script was not very filmic. I know that both Alan Clarke and John Irvin had been approached before me and hadn't found a way of cracking it. I read it and knew immediately it was my meat. It was a satire about politics and bureaucracy. I always liked Stoppard's plays. With this script I felt he hadn't gone far enough and encouraged him to make it more farcical, more surreal. In a way, although this sounds preposterous, it was similar to *Flash Gordon* in that it was a tightrope between farce and serious emotional drama.

"While I was still recovering from surgery and very frail, I didn't let on to the producers, as they wouldn't have given me the job. And this was one film I *had* to make. I knew I was the right person for it even though it would be hard to pull off such a complicated piece in just 24 days, the time allocated to the project."

The title of Stoppard's piece comes from a speech in the script describing Poland's impossible attempt to marry Western freedom with Soviet Communism. "Between August 1980 and December 1981 an attempt was made in Poland to put together two ideas which would not fit," explained Stoppard. "The idea of freedom as it is understood in the West and the idea of socialism as it is understood in the Soviet empire. The attempt failed because it was impossible, in the same sense as it is impossible in geometry to turn a circle into a square."

Prize-winning English actor Bernard Hill (*Boys From the Blackstuff*) was cast in the demanding role of Walesa. "What impressed me about Lech Walesa," says Hill, "is that he always remained so amazingly confident of his knowledge of his fellow Poles. He knew what he wanted for them, and what was right for Poland."

Hill worked extremely hard preparing for the part, following a regime not unlike De Niro's for *Raging Bull* (1980), overeating to put on Walesa's extra weight and immersing himself in literature about Solidarity, watching TV newsreels and videos of the events in Gdansk between August 1980 and December 1981.

Hill was backed by a powerful cast of experienced and well-known stage and screen actors, including RSC actor John Woodvine as Polish party leader Gierek; Richard Kane as General Jaruzelski, Poland's Defence and Prime Minister; Alec McCowen as Rakowski, chief government negotiator with Solidarity; and Frank Middlemass as Brezhnev.

A particular "stroke of genius", according to Stoppard, was Hodges' suggestion to cast the wonderful comedy actor Roy Kinnear as party hack Stanislaw Kania, who briefly became First Secretary of the Polish Communist Party. Kinnear is perfect as the out-of-his-depth bureaucrat trying to stay above water as the pressure piles on.

Stoppard had also incorporated the part of a narrator into the piece, talking to the camera, and had always had himself in mind to take this role on. "Stoppard was the right man for the job," says Hodges. "The piece was like a personal essay and he was perfect for the narrator, but in the end the producers wanted a name actor. Usual story."

Richard Crenna was cast as Narrator. "I don't think I will ever be able to look at Walesa again without imagining that he's really Bernard Hill because he's done such a marvellous job," said Crenna at the time of the film's transmission.

However, although Hill delivers a magnificent central performance, the film was not meant to be the Lech Walesa Story. Although a complex account of that period of time, it is presented in a stylized, semi-theatrical mode that was intended to leave space for viewers to make their own interpretations and draw their own conclusions.

"*Squaring the Circle* is not a filmed play," says Stoppard. "It's not a straight movie, documentary or reconstruction. It's an imaginative view of history."

"My performance wasn't meant to be the definitive film portrait of Walesa," says Hill. "Part of the stylization was me not exactly looking like him or speaking naturalistically as if the Lenin Shipyards were in Liverpool."

In keeping with the highly innovative style of Stoppard's script, all of the action was shot on an impressionistic set created by Polish-born designer Voytek Romain, the Twickenham studio serving as some 20 different locations including Gdansk Shipyard, Red Square, the Politburo and even the Vatican.

"I loved Voytek's work. We'd been friends for years but never worked together before. Coming from Poland he was the obvious choice. I took the script to him, and over a weekend we came up with a plan of how to shoot it. It seemed to me that it was completely ludicrous shooting it on location. Stoppard had written some wonderful complex speeches that I felt had to be delivered uninterrupted. In a studio the actors would be able to deliver his brilliant dialogue without interruptions from the outside world, like aircraft and cars. I knew that if I had to cut into them or change angles they would lose their rhythm. The thrill of the piece was in the language. The actors had to be verbal acrobats. Our job was to provide the circus ring."

Voytek built a large metal gantry with several sets of stairs and gates for access. Into this space he added props as and when necessary for each of the scenes. He laid a circular red carpet, hung crystal chandeliers, and a massive bust of Lenin for the Politburo; with wire mesh and galvanized iron he miraculously transformed the stage into a Warsaw street; and so on. The Warsaw café, where the Narrator sits and a pianist (Vladimir Ashkenazy's son) plays Chopin preludes, was built in an adjacent small studio.

It was, in the words of producer Fred Bogger, "a set as stylized and as exciting as the dramatic concept of the story".

Hodges had difficulty convincing the producers that this was the way to go. They were reluctant to leave the reality of actual locations forgetting that the script itself wasn't realistic. It constantly switched from farce in the scenes with the Communist bureaucracy to emotional engagement in the scenes with Walesa. Voytek's set brilliantly accommodated both farce and realism. Hodges won his argument but with one exception:

"There was a sequence of key scenes throughout the piece, which had Brezhnev meeting the succession of Polish leaders at a beach on the Black Sea. The producers at TVS agreed that we could shoot everything in the studio with the proviso that the beach scenes were shot on location. They could let go of realism – but not quite!

"I knew that the intrusion of a real location would destroy the whole piece, but I agreed! I had a plan that would solve the problem but knew it would frighten the life out of them. So I kept mum.

"With shooting underway it soon became apparent that we wouldn't be able to afford to do it anyway. We only had a 24-day schedule. The beach would be an overnight shoot and we'd have to pay the actors and crew to stay over. Besides I had a much better idea.

"Now my time with Fellini paid off. I had talked to him for hours about *Casanova* (1976) and Donati's contribution. There is a scene when Donald Sutherland as Casanova is rowing across to an island. As *Casanova* was also shot in a studio they had much the same problem as we did. How to create a sea in the studio? They solved it brilliantly with black plastic – it's a night scene – and a wind machine. I knew exactly how to create our beach.

"I had Voytek lay vast sheets of white plastic, ours was a day scene, and run them away from several truckloads of pebbles tipped onto the studio floor and up to a cyclorama. We then shone hard light on to the plastic so that it kicked off it, like the sun does off the sea. Then we brought in a wind machine to make the plastic ripple. Hey presto – we had our beach! And it cost bugger all.

"I hear the film is now used as a model on film courses, although I haven't seen much evidence of its influence just yet! Thanks to Stoppard's script and Voytek's set it was a totally original work."

This Anglo-American co-production between TV South, Metromedia Producers Corporation and Britannic Film and Television took some 18 months and £1.25 million to get off the ground, but only four weeks to shoot. The trans-Atlantic partnership was an uneasy one.

Hodges says the project became an "endless two and a half years" in which Stoppard made several trips to America, shooting extra scenes and editing an American version, which needed to be 10 minutes shorter. In reality, they found it intellectually too demanding for their audiences. They wanted to edit their own "simpler" version. But nobody had told Hodges. The ensuing row led to Hodges refusing to have his name on this version and to Stoppard trying to act as mediator:

"I love Tom Stoppard but he really was naïve in this instance," says Hodges. "The script was brilliant and the Americans knew what they were getting into. It was a very sophisticated work and they were insulting their audience by dumbing it down. Why do they always go for the lowest common denominator? Tom should never have compromised. I fought hard for his script to be made as written."

"Worst of all," Hodges continues, "I turned up early for the music session to find the composer Roy Budd recording a musical theme – a piece of sickly sentimental shit – for an American soundtrack I hadn't been told about. It was being compiled behind my back. Remember that Roy was the composer on *Get Carter*. That hurt. Maybe he didn't know they were deceiving me? I was so busy yelling at the producers I never asked. Deceit is part of all human transactions, it just seems worse in the film business. I've also come across a lot of frightened people who shouldn't be working in it. They have no instinct for it, no belief."

Ironically, it was the British version of *Squaring the Circle,* not the US cut, that won an Emmy. Stoppard flew to New York to collect it; Hodges wasn't invited or even told of the prize. The film also won the Critic's Prize at the Banff Television Festival. Hodges has never seen his 'Rocky', and very nearly didn't see his share of the $10,000 prize. According to Hodges, he would never have known he'd won anything if his old colleague Gus MacDonald hadn't telephoned to congratulate him.

"Soon after Gus rang I went to Vancouver. I contacted the festival organizers in Banff who told me the cash prize had been split between the production designer and the cameraman! The cameraman! I couldn't believe it! I was broke at the time, because of all the tax problems that go with a divorce, and needed the money. Fuck the Rocky! They happily rewrote the cheque and sent it to me. They – whoever 'they' may be – had tried to cheat me right to the end."

Despite the problems, Hodges should certainly be proud of *Squaring the Circle*. An adventurous attempt to rewrite the rules of TV documentary drama, it is proof that innovative television projects can be a success – that TV drama *can* be thought-provoking. Not since Patrick McGoohan's allegory *The Prisoner* – or Dennis Potter's earlier television plays – had a network funded so challenging and radical a project.

THEY CAME, THEY SAW,
THEY DID A LITTLE SHOPPING...

The Alternative Approach:
Morons from Outer Space

They came, they saw, they did a little shopping...
Morons poster tagline

Chapter 8

In 1985, Hodges was approached by an old friend, film producer Verity Lambert, at the time head of production at EMI. She wanted him to take a look at a script written by Mel Smith and Griff Rhys Jones, household names in the UK through the BBC television series *Not The Nine O'clock News.*

"The project initially interested me because I was looking for a base in the UK," explains Hodges. "I wanted to begin working here on a regular basis. EMI was a UK company so I agreed to direct *Morons* if they would finance *Mid-Atlantic*, the screenplay I'd written back in 1975. Verity agreed and I found myself with a two-picture deal. It was too good to be true. And that's exactly what it was!"

Morons from Outer Space began from the premise that extraterrestrials may not be the super-intelligent super-civilized creatures idealistically portrayed in the cinema. What if they have low IQs? Are uncivilized slobs? Complete morons?

Hodges took to this idea with alacrity. The film starts with four inhabitants from the planet of Blob cruising in outer space, holidaying in a decrepit hired spacecraft. They are Bernard (Mel Smith), Desmond Brock (Jimmy Nail), his pretty blonde wife Sandra (Joanne Pearce) and Julian (Paul Bown).

"I'm anti-Spielbergian. Anti his saccharine sentimental take on the world. I liked the idea of directing the antidote."
Mike Hodges

Everything about them, from their gaudy spacecraft to their tacky costumes, suggests a taste for everything moronic, a mirror image of much in our own popular culture. Their *Star Trek*-type cockpit extends into a mock-timbered kitchen worthy of any trailer home. A disembodied female voice reminds them to "Keep Space Tidy. Thank you."

They are lost. While the others discuss a course of action, Bernard goes outside in his spacesuit for a solitary game of spaceball. Desmond, even thicker than the others if that's possible, accidentally

Previous page: the UK poster image for Mike Hodges' 1985 comedy Morons from Outer Space

touches the starter button on the control panel. Their small "podule" detaches itself from the mother ship and zooms away, leaving Bernard forlornly floating alone with his spaceball. Eventually the "podule" crashlands on the M1 motorway in England.

News of their arrival causes panic world-wide. Colonel Laribee (James B Sikking), a flamboyant, fast-talking special attaché to the US Embassy, and Commander Matteson (Dinsdale Landen), a top British security officer, are assigned the task of interrogating Desmond, Sandra and Julian when they emerge from their space capsule.

Graham Sweetley (Griff Rhys Jones), tea boy in a television news bureau, does his best to cover the momentous events (since everyone else is out of the office) and soon becomes heavily involved with the three aliens.

Extensive psychological interviews and physical tests are carried out on the aliens, under the supervision of Laribee and Matteson. The conclusion reached is unanimous and inescapable; they are morons – "pinheads from another planet". Graham Sweetley, however, recognizes their enormous potential in a world obsessed by celebrity. He puts them under contract and is soon selling their life stories to the tabloids, booking them on television talk shows, even turning them into pop superstars.

Meanwhile, Bernard, having hitched a lift with a stray spacecraft only to be rudely ejected, lands in California where he has a bad time trying to explain who he is and where he comes from. Not surprisingly, he's interned in a mental asylum (shades of *One Flew Over the Cuckoo's Nest*) but manages to escape. Reduced to becoming a down-and-out, he eventually makes it to New York. Desmond, Sandra and Julian are there to give a mammoth pop concert at Shea Stadium.

Bernard manages to visit them in their glitzy dressing room. They don't want to know him and have him thrown out. During the concert a spacecraft lands in the stadium. A repo man has come to recover their hired spacecraft. They are forced to return with him to the planet Blob. Bernard watches the spacecraft depart, sad and alone in the empty stadium, as Graham approaches: "Hi Bernard! You don't

know me, but I know who you are. Have a cigar." It's a fat one. Graham can afford it.

Says Hodges: "Of course *Morons from Outer Space* is gross in many ways, but it is 'grossness' that it's satirizing. It certainly encompasses many of my own observations of the world now. The satire is very bitter, Jonathan Swift in a contemporary sleeve. I confess to being anti-Spielbergian, anti his saccharine sentimental take on the world. And I certainly don't go along with the idea that if there is life outside this galaxy it is necessarily more intelligent. You could argue that, if they're on the same trajectory as our civilization only they are historically

Griff Rhys Jones as reporter-turned-showbiz-manager Graham Sweetley in Morons from Outer Space

further along, they could just as easily be dumb, morons. My opinion seesaws on whether we are being 'dumbed' down. In some ways we definitely are: in other ways maybe not. Only time will tell. The race is still on between the ignorant and the bright. Maybe it's a close-run thing, I don't know. In *Morons* it's over.

"Why are we constantly looking for an outside force, a guru, to save us? Whether it's God or ET. I wish we could just grow up and learn to manage without God, ET, or the Queen for that matter. Only then will we get on and help ourselves."

Morons from Outer Space wasn't always a smooth ride. There was a serious glitch about half way into the shoot:

"Mel and Griff were shown a rough cut of the material we'd shot so far. That was a big mistake and caused a lot of unnecessary aggravation. I don't care who you are, it's difficult to assess a rough cut and I don't think Mel and Griff read it right. They found my approach too subtle for populist comedy. And Verity Lambert decided the lighting was too moody, not bright enough for a comedy, and that I was shooting too wide. Sadly, for a variety of reasons, some of the team were elbowed. Both the producer and the production designer were removed, a major upheaval in the middle of the shoot.

"I contemplated resigning but decided against it. I couldn't afford another dispute. I was tired of fighting for the moment. And it wasn't a film that should be taken too seriously. It affected me though. I let certain actors get away with performances that normally I wouldn't have tolerated. *And* I put more light on them which is not my style at all. In the end, *Morons from Outer Space* is awash with caricatures. The aliens, on the other hand, gave brilliantly truthful performances – all of them.

"It was a shame Mel and Griff didn't have more time to work on the script. The idea was so great I kept asking them to take it more seriously. Maybe they didn't *want* to take it seriously? On the other hand maybe I take things too seriously? That said, if there had been more subtlety in the writing, I think it could have been a major comedy – without those OTT performances. But I'm afraid I am guilty of letting it happen."

The idea of *Morons from Outer Space* may be brilliant but it seems the critics missed the point.

"The Americans got it. But I think they're less snobbish about television comedians turning to the cinema. Here in the UK the critics were waiting for Mel and Griff. Not only did they have it in for them

> "Some critics were extremely hateful, one actually declaring, 'Die before you see this film'. I have to admit that's my favourite of all!"
> Mike Hodges

but they resolutely refused to get the idea behind the film. Maybe the title put them off. It was originally called *Illegal Aliens* but was changed during post-production. Some critics were extremely hateful, one actually declaring, 'Die before you see this film'. I have to admit that's my favourite of all!

"Whereas Mel and Griff were shaken by that kind of critical response, after being used to rave reviews for their television work, I was used to it! And besides, I thought, and still think, it is a really well-made film. Money well spent. It's all up there on the screen."

Whatever the shortcomings of *Morons from Outer Space,* it has great production values. Although the humour can be fairly low brow (but not by today's standards), beneath its apparent silliness the film is rife with satire and irony.

The best comic moments come from the early interrogation of the aliens. One of the interrogators has seen *Invasion of the Body Snatchers* too many times, believing their stupidity could be just a mask. With a logic that seems irrefutable to him, he keeps coming up with statements such as: "When you're in the tub, and a man-eating spider crawls out of the faucet, you don't ask him to hand you the soap!" Hodges claims this sequence originally contained questions about democracy on Blob. The morons had no idea how their planet was governed. Sadly they were cut because the sequence was too long.

Chaos reigns surreal throughout *Morons from Outer Space.* Unfortunately the film fails to sustain its basic comic premise for more than the first half of its modest running time. Perhaps the aliens become just too moronic to sustain interest?

After *Morons from Outer Space* was completed, Verity Lambert left her job at EMI. The two-picture deal was never honoured and Hodges never got to make *Mid-Atlantic*. Instead, his first play, *Soft Shoe Shuffle*, a black comedy starring Frances Tomelty, was performed at the Lyric Theatre in Hammersmith. Although a success, it would be another 15 years before Hodges would return to the theatre.

Instead, he went back to filmmaking and agreed to direct two television dramas. The first was a 30-minute episode for *The Hitchhiker* series called *W.G.O.D.* (1985). The second was a feature-length movie called *Florida Straits* (1986), both for HBO.

The Hitchhiker was HBO's first – and most popular – original dramatic series and won eight ACE Awards to become the highest-ranking series on pay television. Presenting sophisticated tales of terror, horror and suspense, the series debuted in November 1983. The show was not only at the forefront of original programming for cable, but also helped establish the standards of excellence for such programming. The series also helped establish the acceptance of cable programming as an avenue for top film and television talents, and ran until February 1991.

This half-hour dramatic anthology series presented modern morality tales with contemporary players. In 85 chilling stories, men and women struggle with the best and worst in themselves, battling with – and all too often succumbing to – their deepest lusts, obsessions and fears. With powerful and controversial adult productions, the series' tales of terror were infused with stunning film-noir production values and movie-marquee talent.

The compelling mini-features attracted an impressive, international roster of film talent, both in front of and behind the camera, resulting in tremendous popularity and critical acclaim. In its 10 years, *The Hitchhiker* attracted the talents of directors and actors, including Paul Verhoeven, Philip Noyce, Daniel Vigne, Willem Dafoe, Kirstie Alley, Page Fletcher, Peter Coyote, Virginia Madsen, Gary Busey, Ken Olin, Micheal O'Keefe and Elliot Gould, and brought feature film production values to television.

Attracted by the prestigious nature of the project, Hodges signed up to direct Tom Baum's teleplay entitled *W.G.O.D.* in which Reverend

Nolan Powers (Gary Busey), a money-hungry radio evangelist preaches on the air waves about the Bible. "The airwaves belong to God on 1350 AM," he booms, before taking calls live on air for those needing to confess.

"God sees you," he says to a woman needing advice on her private life. "Dump this turkey!"

But the comments from the Hitchhiker (Page Fletcher) at the start of the episode are all too telling: "A confession is good for the soul. If you're the Reverend Nolan Powers it's also good for business. But no matter how big he is there's one caller out there he doesn't want to hear from …"

Soon afterwards, live on air, Powers gets a call from a man who says the Reverend is "afraid of the truth". When asked what his favourite song is, the voice replies, "What a Friend You Have in Jesus".

Show over, the Reverend drives home to his tacky mansion. As it happens his mother (Geraldine Page) is listening to a recording by his dead brother. The song is "What a Friend You Have in Jesus". Although he is a good son, she tells him, his younger brother (who vanished years ago) was perfect.

Tabloid news reporter, Harry Sato (Robert Ito), picks up on the story about Gerald's mysterious disappearance and starts to investigate.

During the Powers radio show the following day, the anonymous voice calls again and Powers rudely cuts him off. Completely crazed, Powers drives, in the lashing rain, to a find a grave. He starts digging frantically. The voice, fading in and out wherever he is, forces him back into the studio. There, in a complete breakdown, he admits to killing his brother out of jealousy for his mother's love. Suddenly, he realizes his confessions have been transmitted live on air. The film closes with the Hitchhiker's closing comments: "The Reverend Powers had a long-buried secret, testament to his envy and wrath. But when he consecrated his tower of power, he also gave a voice to his unholy past."

The focus on fundamentalist religion and its power in America today was of obvious interest to Hodges, who was offered a choice of several half-hour scripts. In the original screenplay, during Powers's battle with the voice of his brother, he starts getting electric shocks from the microphone. Hodges immediately changed this sequence: "Religion is about blood. So instead of electric shocks I had blood dripping from the microphone and oozing from the soundproofing. The walls even start heaving. It was like a Francis Bacon painting!"

Shortly after the transmission of *W.G.O.D.*, Hodges signed up for the next HBO project, the feature-length TV movie called *Florida Straits*.

The film is set 20 years after the Bay of Pigs invasion. Carlos Jayne (Raul Julia) persuades Lucky Boone (Fred Ward) and Mac (Daniel Jenkins) to sail their fishing boat into Cuba where a fortune in gold bullion had been buried during the abortive 1961 military action.

Their daring trek to the mountains of Cuba takes them to a huge abandoned power station described as "the ruins of an ancient empire… initially funded by the Batista government, but abandoned when Castro took power". They are captured by El Gato and his band of rebels but manage to escape.

Carlos leads them to the gold but then insists they wait while he finds Carmen, the real reason for his return to Cuba. But Carmen has made a new life for herself, even marrying a police officer. Her husband agrees to turn a blind eye if he leaves immediately.

Carlos does just that. He, Mac and Lucky head back to the boat. El Gato reappears but Lucky lures him into a minefield and to his death. The trio, now at sea, are spotted by Cuban patrol boats. Carlos is shot and the boat badly damaged. But Mac and Lucky are rescued. And so is most of the gold.

The script wasn't brilliant but Hodges took the job. He needed to earn some money and the film was to be shot in Mexico, a country he loved.

"Off I went to Mexico, had a great time choosing the locations and returned thinking I could make the script work. With Fred Ward and Raul Julia on board, I thought to myself this might not be so bad after all.

"Next thing the phone rings. It's the producers calling to say they don't want me to shoot in Mexico after all because they can't afford it! I never heard anybody say they couldn't afford to shoot in Mexico. Instead, they tell me they want it shot in North Carolina. I couldn't believe it. The whole story takes place in the jungle! North Carolina is more like Dorset! To this day I'm not sure what the real story was. You can be sure it's not a pretty one. Lies and deceit stalking me again. I would love to have told them there and then to stuff it but I couldn't afford to.

"So I fly out to Charlotte in North Carolina and they drive me to a little town called Shelby. This place is like *Peyton Place*! It turns out they'd done some stupid deal with a production studio there. It was a complete nightmare! And I was stuck in this place for six months. I had committed myself contractually.

"Luckily, I got to bring over my own team, which included Voytek (*Squaring the Circle*), the cameraman, focus puller, editor and even my two sons. The crew were brilliant and we just about pulled it off.

"I came back, edited it, delivered it to HBO and thought that was the end of it. I should be so lucky! The producer then decides he wanted to re-cut the film, even though HBO had been happy with it. The Directors' Guild of America intervened on my behalf but, when he fired my editor, there was nothing I could do but return to England.

"I learned later they had shot additional scenes with a double of Raul Julia, a man half his size and wearing a terrible wig. Worse still they had ladled some awful music all over it, throwing out all the amazing Cuban music I'd found in New York. This piece of garbage was shown on HBO. Later it was even released in France as a feature film, and with my name on it. But I had the last laugh. The Directors' Guild of America traced this release and the producers were made to pay me a substantial sum of money as compensation."

That wasn't the only good thing to have come out of *Florida Straits*. It took him to North Carolina and it was there that the creative seeds for *Black Rainbow* were sown. He began writing it immediately after he got back to Britain. But before it could be made, Hodges had another offer ...

Cut and Trust:
A Prayer for the Dying

"Many films are pre-sold around the world. But are
these people selling what the filmmakers are making?
And if it's pre-sold, how can a film have the
spontaneous life on which all art is based?"
Mike Hodges

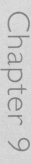

Chapter 9

The year 1986 began with the debacle that was *Florida Straits*. On his return from America, Hodges was asked to direct a screenplay based on the Jack Higgins' novel, *A Prayer for the Dying*. First-choice director, Franc Roddam, had walked only weeks before the offer came. According to the producers he had rewritten the screenplay, turning it into an "extremely violent" version, which was not to their liking. "Quite right," explains Hodges, "the whole point of *A Prayer for the Dying* is that it is about a man turning his back on violence."

Time wasn't on Hodges' side. The normal pre-production period is eight weeks; he had four. The producers had a million-dollar pay-or-play deal with Mickey Rourke and he had another film tied in to his busy schedule further down the line. They had no other actors signed up.

"On the walls of most film production offices is a supposedly humorous poster entitled, 'The Six Stages of Production'. Stage One is listed as 'Wild Enthusiasm'. Stage Six as 'Promotion of the Incompetent'. Heavy-handed humour sadly based on fact. It was

"This was anthropological work." Mike Hodges

Stage One for me in August 1986, and producers Sam Goldwyn Jr and Peter Snell did seem enthusiastic when I agreed to take on the project. 'Wild' enthusiasm would be an exaggeration, but they were mighty relieved. Maybe it was because Rourke had to be paid one million buckeroos whether the movie was made or not, and it had to be finished within 12 weeks. A tall order, especially when the script needed re-writing, locations had to be found, crew chosen and 60-odd actors cast.

"So why did I take such an enormous professional risk? Money (I was still in the divorce trap), Mickey Rourke (I really liked his work), excitement – and subject matter. It was in my manor. I'd already made a successful gangster film. I'm fascinated by the antics of funeral directors, having made a documentary about them for *World In Action*. And I am a lapsed Catholic. This was anthropological work.

Previous page: in Silvertown for Hodges' controversial 1987 film A Prayer for the Dying. Camera operator Gordon Haymen (bearded) and cinematographer, Mike Garfath, on the left; both longtime collaborators with Hodges

"The advantage of having to work quickly is that you operate totally on instinct. Firstly, I persuaded Bob Hoskins and Alan Bates to do a script they both found unappealing, by reversing the obvious; offering Bob the role of the Catholic priest, Alan the funeral undertaker gang boss. I also pruned the violence to a minimum. That done, I was able to provide the proper frame for Rourke's characterization – on which he had done considerable work, much of it painful. He's an actor who has to experience the actuality; for example, Martin Fallon had a tattoo. He could easily have had a transfer but Mickey insisted on a real one. Sadly, it went septic, presaging the film's fate. Of course, we didn't know that then."

A Prayer for the Dying was shot on location in Silvertown, East London. It went smoothly and the finished film was delivered on time and on budget to Goldwyn. There was, however, one major glitch; the American producers hated Rourke's performance, and Rourke took an instant dislike to their locum. He had him banned from the set.

The film opens with the view of a narrow country road in Northern Ireland. IRA man Martin Fallon (Mickey Rourke) watches from a wood above as his team rigs a bomb. It is intended for a convoy of British army trucks scheduled to pass. As they approach they pull to the side, allowing a school bus full of kids to pass them. A mortified Fallon can only watch as the bus explodes.

The scene shifts to London, where the rest of the action is set. Local crime boss Jack Meehan (Alan Bates) wants Fallon, now on the run, to kill a prominent rival hood named Kristou. In exchange, he will be given $50,000, a new passport and the chance of a new life in America. Fallon initially declines. Damaged spiritually by his murderous work for the "glorious cause", he wants no more of killing. "I never killed for money, or because I enjoyed it," he says. When he learns that IRA agents Liam Docherty (Liam Neeson) and Siobhan Donovan (Alison Doody) have come after him for "desertion", he agrees to the deal. Useless to his cause, hunted by police and IRA, he's left with no choice – it's either kill Kristou or be killed.

Disguised as a Roman Catholic priest, Fallon tracks Kristou to a cemetery. He kills him beside a relative's grave. Seen by a local priest, Fr Da Costa (Bob Hoskins), Fallon silences him by confessing

to the murder, sealing his lips under the pact of the confessional. Fallon also meets the priest's blind niece, Anna (Sammi Davis), who, of course, falls in love with him. Fallon takes her to the local funfair, watched from a distance by Meehan's thuggish brother Billy. Fallon leaves her at the presbytery not knowing that Billy is waiting inside. When he attempts to rape Anna, she stabs him with a pair of scissors.

Eventually Fallon is tracked down by Docherty, but he cannot bring himself to shoot his friend. This failure costs him his own life. Donovan executes him. Angry that Fallon has not disposed of the priest, Meehan ambushes him aboard the ship taking him to the US. His master plan includes blowing up Da Costa and Anna with a bomb, designed to implicate the IRA. But Fallon escapes the trap,

Hodges and Rourke with the completion bond broker, who guarantees to finance the completion of a film should something go wrong

reaching the church before the bomb goes off. He confronts Meehan with the news of his brother's death, and frees Anna and Da Costa. In the ensuing struggle, the bomb detonates. Meehan is killed and Fallon mortally wounded. Before he dies, trapped under debris, Da Costa recites "a prayer for the dying".

Rourke is a compelling figure. His performance as a man caught in a moral dilemma is fascinating to watch. Whenever he's on screen, an air of tension surrounds him. Bates, too, seems to take particular pleasure in playing the amoral sadistic mobster who, conveniently, also owns a funeral parlour.

The film returns to many of Hodges' constant themes. Religious imagery is present throughout – even in the cut that was released. *A Prayer for the Dying* is replete with an almost biblical blind person, a statue of the Virgin Mary spattered with blood, and a massive crucifix falling from the church ceiling. In the film's finale Fallon clings to the figure of Christ before both crash to the floor, ending up as a pile of rubble, much like his own faith had 40 years before.

Despite Hodges delivering what he thought was an efficient, gripping film to Goldwyn, it was taken to America and completely re-edited. Even Jon Scott's minimal score was replaced with Bill Conti's sickly-sentimental cod-Irish soundtrack.

"I had really enjoyed making the film and thought Mickey Rourke was just great in it. He had mastered the Belfast accent brilliantly, no easy job, and I thought we'd pulled it off. Again, I was wrong.

"I remember Goldwyn Jr telephoning just two days into shooting to ask how I was doing. I replied, 'It's like surfing!' He laughed. I never heard him laugh again.

"The first intimation that we were making something beyond the ken of our American producers arrived by telex. They hated Rourke's performance, describing it as 'listless'. As further encouragement, they sent another telex suggesting he be replaced because he was mentally and physically incapable of performing the role. As Rourke's characterization was based on a man having a breakdown, having lost his beliefs, their opinion was a triumphant endorsement of an extraordinary performance. Sadly, they didn't see it that way. They imagined the IRA more as Mafia hit men, cross-fertilized with the heroes of Kung Fu movies. The realization that we were making different films dropped like a hand grenade. Only it didn't explode for some months.

"... the director has to encompass the whole film in his mind, that's his job. He has to stand firm while others have doubts, or the whole edifice will collapse." Mike Hodges

"The problem is always the same in filmmaking. How do you get everybody involved to synchronize? The answer is, you can't. You hope that when the jigsaw puzzle is finally put together, they will get the picture, so to speak. It's an act of faith. But the problem of a united vision goes beyond even the makers, to the sales force. Many films are pre-sold around the world. But are these people selling what the filmmakers are making? And if it's pre-sold, how can a film have the spontaneous life on which all art is based?

"Of one thing you can be sure, the director has to encompass the whole film in his mind, that's his job. He has to stand firm while others have doubts, or the whole edifice will collapse. I completed *A Prayer for the Dying* in December 1986, on time and on budget. Some weeks later, I was recording organ music for the soundtrack. We were in St Paul's, the actors' church in Bedford Street, and I was looking at the commemorative plaques. One read, 'Foolery, sir, does walk the orb. Like the sun it shines everywhere.' Another portent? Soon afterwards, my version of the film was delivered to, and aborted by, Sam Goldwyn Jr in sunny Los Angeles.

"It's an often-forgotten fact that a film is simply a juxtaposition of images and sounds; the order of which is decided by the director, together with his or her editor. It is then shown to the producer, and amended until both are satisfied with the cut. Previews with test audiences follow, so that the final version can be verified before cutting the negative. If the director is not allowed to control the order of the images and sounds he or she has created, then that person can no longer be considered the director. I don't have to remind anyone of the fate meted out to Orson Welles, Von Stroheim, Keaton and many other cinema luminaries. This struggle for creative freedom has been a long and bloody one.

"In July 1987, five months after I delivered my version of the film, I was finally shown what Goldwyn Jr had perpetrated in my name. The film had been completely re-edited, and a different music and soundtrack substituted. The atmosphere was all gone – they went for mundane storytelling with the pace of a TV serial. I hated it. It was no longer the film I had made. Worse, that trust between director and actor, in this case Hoskins and Bates, had been

Hodges with production supervisor Christabel Albery

breached. The role of Da Costa suffered the worst. Whilst the film released is not a totally awful film, it is nothing like the film I delivered.

"Goldwyn Jr later excused himself by saying that the film was now 'more acceptable to American audiences'. Later he made me choke over my breakfast when, in a Sunday broadsheet, he is quoted as saying: 'My crusade has always been to make British filmmakers believe in themselves, rather than to ape the American market.'"

Hodges washed his hands of the whole affair, publicly disowning the film after the producers refused to remove his name. "I often wonder if American audiences realize what is done in their name," asks Hodges. "*A Prayer for the Dying* was one of many of my films to have been tampered with 'in their name'. I think they would be deeply insulted."

Hodges' public condemnation attracted widespread coverage, across all media. This was mainly due to a press release Hodges' put together through the PR company Sue Rolfe Associates, with the headline "Mike Hodges Disowns A Prayer For The Dying". This news release read:

Press Release
"Film director Mike Hodges completed the film *A Prayer for the Dying* for Samuel Goldwyn in February this year. Since then the first opportunity Hodges was given to view the final version was on Tuesday 14th July. He was appalled by what he saw and immediately demanded that his name be removed from the credits. Hoskins and Bates having seen Hodges version asked Goldwyn to change it but to no avail. Mickey Rourke has already disowned the film. *A Prayer for the Dying* is due to open in America on August 28th. Peter Snell, the producer, refused to remove Hodges name from the film despite the fact

that he had always insisted that he would
have the right to do so should he wish."

This press release was originally intended for the trade papers, such as *Variety* and *The Hollywood Reporter*. However, it was released to all UK national newspapers. Somehow a rumour began to circulate that Hodges' version had been re-edited without his consent because it had a pro-IRA ending – a serious allegation implying he was sympathetic to that cause. Hodges responded in an open letter to the *Daily Telegraph*: "Let me make it clear, *A Prayer for the Dying* is the story of a man who has defected from the IRA, sickened by the use of violence. It is simply not possible for *any* version of the film to be pro-IRA. Even my adversaries in this dispute would agree with that."

The storm that surrounded the film was similar to the subject of his second film *Rumour*. The irony of this didn't go unnoticed by Hodges: "Now I really knew what it was like to be set on by the rat pack. I wouldn't recommend it to anyone. The lies and the ignorance undermines any belief system you may have left."

This was the third film in a row to be taken away from Hodges and re-cut without his approval, something which angered him greatly. "After going public," he explains, "no one in the industry wanted to know about me. Defend your films and you risk being branded as 'difficult'. Be passionate about them and you're vulnerable. I learnt that throughout the 1980s."

Not many people have seen the original director's cut of *A Prayer for the Dying*. It is certainly a different movie: different in mood. A weird concoction of religion, politics and gothic melodrama, it is very much a mainstream movie.

Interestingly, the director's cut of *A Prayer for the Dying* may well find an audience after all. Hodges has been in talks with MGM, which now own the rights, to restore the film to its original form for a special-edition DVD release. "The material they cut must be sitting on a shelf somewhere," says Hodges. "It's just a matter of tracking it down. I would really love to see it released in its proper form. Will we keep Sam Goldwyn Jr's name on it I wonder?"

After the ordeal of *A Prayer for the Dying*, some close friends

approached Hodges to write a script based on events surrounding the controversial 1937 musical drama, *The Cradle Will Rock*. It was written by Marc Blitzstein and directed by the 22-year-old Orson Welles. Very influenced by Bertolt Brecht, the setting was an American steel town. The subject was the exploitation of the workers, and prostitution at every level. When word got out that the musical was an attack on capitalism, resources from the New Deal funding were cut off and they were even denied use of the theatre. On the opening night Orson Welles and John Houseman, the producer, moved the show (and the audience) 20 blocks up Broadway. There it was performed without scenery, props or costumes. "Instead of breaking under political pressure," explains Hodges, "they just took the show to another venue. The only problem was that the cast couldn't legally appear on stage as they were under contract. John Houseman realized that, under the American Constitution, nobody could stop them joining in the

Director and star of A Prayer for the Dying relax during the shoot

musical from among the audience." This they did and the play was a hit. It ran for three months.

"I agreed to write this piece with the proviso that all the characters were not Welles and Houseman but actors 'pretending' to be Welles, Houseman and the others. I set all the action in a theatre and, as in *Squaring the Circle*, had characters talking to camera, in this case two stage hands.

"My finished script was good enough to attract Tim Robbins as Orson Welles, Jeff Goldblum as Marc Blitzstein and Alan Rickman as John Houseman. But sadly it was a bit too off the wall for the money men, and, at the time, this cast was relatively unknown. We didn't get the finance.

"A few years later, I was in Los Angeles, visiting Bob Altman on the set of *The Player*. It was at this point I actually met Tim Robbins for the first time, as up until then our dealings had been through his agent. When I was introduced to him, I asked if he remembered my script, which I'd been calling *Midnight Shakes the Memory*. He told me how much he liked it and that he still kept a copy at home!

"Cut to the chase! When he became a major star because of *The Player*, and Alan Rickman's career took off with *Truly, Madly, Deeply*, I suggested we try to get financial backing once more.

"Not surprisingly, the Houseman role was now too small for Alan. And when they approached Robbins he said 'yes', but wanted to write and direct it himself. I stepped aside immediately, knowing full well that with his name attached to it, it would be made.

"I had written the original script for a token $10,000 and assumed I would now be paid a proper fee for my work. Wrong again!

"I'd used a paragraph from Houseman's biography in my script and required permission to use it. Houseman read it just before he died and approved – but we still had to pay $10,000 for the rights. The producers, however, could only afford $5,000 – so I gave half of my fee straight back! Now, years later, they were expecting me to simply sign over my rights so that Robbins could make his film. And for this they offered to repay me the $5,000. This time around I wasn't prepared to be screwed and made sure they paid a substantial fee for my work. Robbins' film was a properly funded big-budget film with lots of stars. They could afford to pay me properly but, needless to say, they tried not to."

Tim Robbins took over the project, turning it into a tapestry of interwoven stories far removed from the original story: Nelson Rockefeller (John Cusack) commissions Mexican artist Diego Rivera (Ruben Blades) to paint the lobby of Rockefeller Center, while Italian propagandist Margherita Sarfatti (Susan Sarandon) sells Da Vincis to millionaires to fund the Mussolini war effort. A paranoid ventriloquist (Bill Murray) tries to rid his vaudeville troupe of communists, and a 22-year-old Orson Welles (Angus MacFadyen) directs his Federal Theater group in an infamous stage production of *The Cradle Will Rock*, which is closed down on the eve of its opening by US soldiers. The film, which he called *The Cradle Will Rock* (1999) also stars Hank Azaria, Joan Cusack, Cary Elwes, Philip Baker Hall, Cherry Jones, Vanessa Redgrave, John Turturro, and Emily Watson.

Hodges received no credit on Robbins' film – and says he wouldn't want one:

"It was a mess. I thought it was pretentious twaddle. He over-complicated a wonderfully simple storyline by filling the film with superfluous posturing characters like Rockefeller and Diego Rivera – presumably to cast it up with famous people. He literally lost the plot, which was a great shame. What I had written originally was so simple and I believe simplicity is the key to everything."

Faith and Fakery:
Black Rainbow

"Kudzu. Goddamned kudzu. You know we can't
kill that stuff. Nothing known to man can stop it.
Poisons. Pesticides. They even tried flame-throwers."
From the opening scene in *Black Rainbow*

Chapter 10

Hodges wrote *Black Rainbow* on spec. On completing the screenplay he gave it to his agent Terence Baker who in turn passed it on to John Quested, the head of Goldcrest Films. He had acquired the company when it had gone to the wall with Hugh Hudson's *Revolution*.

"Terence was in a meeting with Quested trying to find out what sort of projects Goldcrest were after and John said that they wanted something like *Elmer Gantry*, something in the same vein as the old Jean Simmons/Burt Lancaster film about an evangelist preacher, which John loved. Of course, Terence was able to say he had just the script – *Black Rainbow*!

The genesis of the piece was odd. I had wanted to write, quite simply, about the way we're fucking up this planet. Only fools can't see that what we're doing is not only crassly ignorant and arrogant – but unnecessary. I desperately wanted to write about that. So I wrote *Black Rainbow*."

But Hodges wasn't interested in some clichéd scenario of a world on the brink of meltdown, or a nuclear-based thriller, so he looked for something more original.

His distrust of American fundamentalist preachers had already shown up in the 1985 HBO drama *W.G.O.D.* In *Black Rainbow*, Hodges casts the net wider, setting this supernatural thriller in the Bible belt, in the underbelly of crumbling industrial towns inhabited by poor folks with a deep-rooted faith in a life after death. There sure had to be one better than this one.

The film opens as the reporter of small-time newspaper *The Oakville Bee*, Gary Wallace (Tom Hulce), tracks down a travelling clairvoyant called Martha Travis (Rosanna Arquette). He finds her in an unnamed rural Southern town after years of searching for her. She had disappeared after the murder of her father – which Gary covered – and the locals in town say, since she moved there 10 years ago and because no one has spoken to her, she's probably a ghost. Gary goes out to her shack and secretly photographs her before knocking on the door. She slams it in his face and we flashback 10 years.

Martha and her drunken father Walter (Jason Robards) are on a train, travelling to the next venue for her performance as a medium.

Previous page: *Kudzu weed – nothing known to man can stop it*

In halls around the South she puts audiences in touch with their relatives on "the other side".

At that night's well-attended show (we see Walter counting the "take") she predicts the murder of a union organizer, Tom Kuron. Kuron, it transpires, is about to blow the whistle on safety and environmental breaches at a chemical plant in Oakville. The next day, when the murder has happened as she has predicted, the sceptical young Gary is sent by his editor to interview her and find out if she's a fraud. Gary arrives at the next town on Martha's itinerary, meets Walter, gets him drunk, and beds Martha in a bid to extract information on the story. We now learn that the owner of the chemical works and the town's main employer is the devout churchgoer Ted Silas (John Bennes). Silas hired a hit man, Lloyd Harley (Mark Joy) from Chicago, to kill Tom Kuron. It's also revealed that the Jewish police chief, Irving Weinberg (Ron Rosenthal), knew about the hit and covered it up to protect Silas.

But the heart of the story is with Martha. Her communications with the dead, which she may have faked for years (we never know), suddenly become increasingly real as she predicts deaths before they actually happen. She has moved from medium to prophet, a prophet of doom. The "rainbow" visions she used to see have turned black, and despair drives her close to madness. Walter, ever the hard-nosed manager, tells her to remember her act is only entertainment, but she swears she can really see the horrors of the future.

At another session, Martha foresees the death of six men. Again her prophecy is later fulfilled by an accident at the local nuclear-fuel plant.

Harley, the hit man, is now on her trail. He waits patiently in her hotel room, ready for her return from the hall. But during her performance that night she foresees Walter's death, and panics. Back in the hotel Harley shoots at a ghostly Martha, apparently escorting her father as he tries to escape. He kills Walter and, in the ensuing shoot-out with the cops, he shoots Weinberg before dying himself in a hail of bullets. Now alone in the hall, Martha dematerializes. The flashback ends.

Back to the present day and Gary is delivering the photographs of the now reclusive Martha, insisting he has a great scoop. His editor is nonplussed. The pictures reveal only a weed-covered shack … and no Martha. The weed has almost totally eliminated any evidence of human existence. It's kudzu, goddamned kudzu. Nothing can destroy it. We're back where we started.

This stimulating film is superbly paced, builds to a powerful climax and plays up the ambiguity of the story in an engaging way. It is delicate, haunting and grossly underrated; and it certainly would have worked better at the box office if it had been handled properly.

Rosanna Arquette is excellent in an understated performance. She brings a vulnerability to her performance and carries off a difficult role with more style and conviction than any of her previous performances had even hinted at. A brilliant role for a woman, Hodges actually had trouble casting the part. "I had a terrible time getting anyone to play Martha," he says. "Eventually Rosanna read the script and, thanks to Martin Scorsese, who had worked with her, she took it straight away."

Robards also brings real on-screen class to the picture and a certain sense of tragic power to his role. "I loved working with Jason," admits Hodges. "He was perfect for the role. In fact, the players were from very different backgrounds – Rosanna from the newer school of American acting, which I'd already experienced with Mickey Rourke, where they have to put themselves into the situation of the character. And then you have actors like Jason Robards, from the old school, who would say: 'You don't put yourself in the position of the character, you just become the character – you don't feel what the character says, the character feels.'"

It was an argument over acting styles that nearly threatened the whole production. Arquette had prepared for her role with a real-life psychic called Laura Day, and an acting coach, Susan Batson. Hodges wasn't aware of this and it led to a severe falling out over a key sequence. "When we were filming 'the act' Rosanna was emoting all over the place," says Hodges. "In fairness she was doing what I had written but it simply wasn't working. It was terrible. I didn't sleep a wink that night. I knew it was no good without even looking at the rushes. In the end there wasn't a single frame I could use. I went to her trailer the following morning. She took one look at me and said, 'You want to re-shoot the scene, don't you?' There was a terrible row, the trailer must have been rocking all over the place. I just turned and said 'think about it' and went outside looking for the producer. Of course they're never around when you need them, so I went back in and we managed to sort things out without him."

"I was so upset," remembers Arquette. "I couldn't believe English filmmakers could be so afraid of emotion and feelings! I thought I was *so* right but in the end I just said okay, I am going to trust you – I am going to trust my director, and we did it his way. And boy was

" I was so upset," remembers Arquette. "I couldn't believe English filmmakers could be so afraid of emotion and feelings! I thought I was so right but in the end I just said okay, I am going to trust you – I am going to trust my director, and we did it his way. And boy was he right. "

he right. He was so, so right. Thank God I trusted him! But that is creative conflict; you have to make things churn a bit to make things real! And besides, it was mostly a good experience. I really wanted to do this movie and loved the script."

Hodges' initial ideas for the screenplay came during *Florida Straits* three years earlier:

"While I was in North Carolina shooting *Florida Straits*, I fell in love with the area – the towns and countryside seemed to bring me back to the paintings of Edward Hopper. When I returned to actually shoot *Black Rainbow*, I was devastated to find that many of the lovely buildings I'd seen had been demolished. Eventually I had to build the hotel rooms because the real ones had gone. The buildings had been ripped down with seemingly no regret on behalf of the inhabitants. The town [Charlotte] as I knew it three years before had almost vanished! So in the film, when Jason Robards turns and says, 'I see

the developers have arrived!' it's for real. The local woman says,
'They're tearing our heart out, Mr Travis!' and he replies, 'It's not
your heart they're after, it's your memories.' Weirdly that was
already in the script. It must have been a premonition, so Charlotte
turned out to be the perfect location for this film. It represents the
wilful destruction of our planet, our cities – and our memories.

"Like in *Get Carter,* I had caught a town losing its identity. As with
Newcastle I was nearly too late.

"While working in North Carolina the first time I began to note
newspaper stories about workers, a foreman or even an inspector
responsible for the reporting of factory health and safety

*Tom Hulce as small-
town reporter Gary
Wallace in* Black
Rainbow *(1990)*

regulations, had been beaten up or murdered. Without exception it was to silence them.

"But as well as wanting to write about this kind of abuse, I wanted to tie it up with the abuse of our natural resources. I wanted to include elements about the perversion of science. I mean, scientists are like children. They want to play with fire. Look what's happening in genetics? Have they thought the consequences through? They certainly didn't with nuclear power. Scientists are driven by ambition to continually advance their particular field, and this need may well destroy us eventually. Maybe it's inevitable.

"Despite losing my faith when I was very young I am still fascinated by religions. In the mainstream religions – Christianity, Islam or Hinduism – I can see few admonitions to preserve the planet, which, if you believe in God, was given to us in sacred trust.

"Older cultures, like the American Indians, the Aborigines, treat the planet with great care. Whatever they took from it, even the smallest thing, they asked for it to be replenished. The places where they live, the plants and animals, everything is treated with respect.

"In the latter-day religions, and in most of our materialist thinking, we've lost our way. I wanted to risk making a film on just that.

"So I needed a character who was a seer, someone who could warn us of the consequences of what we are doing. That's when I came up with the idea of a medium – someone who could be a fraud or might have a genuine gift. Let the observers decide for themselves. That really appealed to me. Someone who supposedly communicates with the dead, which, in a sense, we all do.

"Martha Travis ends up as a prophet of the future. Prophets were often emotionally unstable people and this woman is lonely, unstable, she's unhappy and has slipped into another time scale. This is suggested at the beginning of the film, where time changes for her, as she advances ahead in time. I use the clumsy device of having her make two corrections to her watch. Time is a human device, created to regulate us, imprison us. There was a curious ritual, no longer observed, that when you turned 21, you were given a watch. And of course the watch is a shackle, demanding we pay attention to time."

Hodges says that many viewers of the film seemed to think that, through the character of Martha, he was trying to suggest the existence of an afterlife. Not so, he claims, preferring to think that after death no more than "some kind of psychic residue" remains.

"I found a great symbol to put in the film. In my constant travels around America, I came across the Kudzu weed many times. It was introduced from Japan as a binding agent for the railway tracks, and is almost impossible to destroy. In the Southern States they call it 'foot-a-day' because it spreads so rapidly.

"This weed pleased me immensely whenever I saw it. The way it just spreads itself everywhere, climbing over telegraph poles, over houses – anywhere it wants. It's quite amazing this stuff. It cheered me up because it's the 'wild' saying 'fuck you, you little arseholes – you really don't know what the hell you're doing!' This weed takes over everything. It's as if we've never existed. We haven't found anything that will destroy this stuff."

Kudzu therefore became the film's central metaphor for the constant recycling of the "life force".

Sensitively directed, in *Black Rainbow* Hodges is again questioning religion: "If we didn't believe in all that crap about the hereafter," says a woman whose husband is killed in the chemical plant explosion, "maybe we'd pay more attention to what's going on down here."

Similarly, Martha's mournful lament on the state of the human condition is also effective in highlighting this theme in Hodges' script:

"Why does everything serious have to be turned into entertainment? Politics, wars, famines, space shuttles … they're all just variety acts on TV… I don't see over there at the end of the rainbow any longer. Instead I see wasting diseases, cancers … symptoms of our own self destruction. It haunts me. And it's getting worse. We don't understand what we're doing."

And Martha is quick to explain why everything is turned into an entertainment today: "It's so obvious. It's the only way people can make sense of the random stupidity of it all." When queried by Gary about why she only has one-night-stands, Martha laughs: "This way men lie *with* me and not *to* me."

Earlier in the film, at breakfast, a sweet little girl asks her dad: "What's the population of the world?" "Too many," replies the hit man as he waits for his next assignment. This is pure tongue-in-cheek Hodges and could so easily have come straight from his first theatrical release *Get Carter*, that masterpiece of vitriolic lines. But this isn't Newcastle and we've moved on nearly two decades. Nevertheless, we *are* still in a lousy world. Hodges is fond of quoting Joseph Conrad: "'I have never been able to find in any man's book or any man's talk anything convincing enough to stand up for a moment against my deep-seated sense of fatality governing this man-inhabited world.' I only wish I could put it so succinctly."

Filmed on location in North Carolina in just six weeks with a budget of $7 million, *Black Rainbow* proved what Hodges could do without interference.

Unfortunately, the film was dogged by distribution problems, both in the UK and the US. Despite fantastic reviews, it was quickly dumped by Palace Pictures, after a small, token theatrical release, because the company was going broke, something Hodges hadn't realized. "They needed cash quickly," explains Hodges, "so they sold it to a video company. Although I had delivered the film exactly how I wanted it, it never got the right distribution."

Black Rainbow wasn't released at all in America, going straight to cable television. Miramax, the US distributors, were also going through financial difficulties and needed a cash fix.

It did, however, win Best Screenplay award at the 22nd Sitges Fantasy Film Festival and Best Film at Oporto, where Arquette also won Best Actress. The film has garnered more rave reviews over the years through special screenings. In fact, it eventually reached that substantial cinema audience Hodges had hoped for. When he was working on the music for *Croupier* at Simon Fisher Turner's flat in Brixton, Hodges met a Japanese musician friend of the composer. He left, then came back, very excited, having discovered he had met the director of *Black Rainbow*. "He said, 'I see *Black Rainbow* six times,'" beams Hodges. "And I said, 'on television?' because I assumed he must have either seen it on cable or video. 'No – in the cinema,' he said. 'Very big in Japan.'"

"No one told me it was big in Japan," claims Hodges. "This film had drifted East, without me knowing, landing there like a message in a bottle. I can see why they would like it because it's a sort of ghost story. The Japanese like ghost stories."

Original and intelligent, this was Hodges' finest film since *The Terminal Man* and recaptured some of the grit of *Get Carter* and *Pulp*. In *Black Rainbow*, he made a film in which he managed to blend his hatred of exploitative religions with his socialist politics.

Black Rainbow is a remarkable genre-buster that would have simply bewildered the average *Rambo*-loving 1980s' cinema-goer.

Turned on by Television:
Dandelion Dead and the Healer

Dandelion Dead and the Healer

"Nowadays, television executives are obsessed with
getting name actors in even the small roles.
It's like directing in Madame Tussauds."
Mike Hodges

Chapter 11

After *Black Rainbow*, Hodges couldn't make up his mind what to do next. Something drew him into contemplating writing another Chabrolesque thriller, as he had done with *Suspect* in 1969.

"For some reason I had started reading the books of Georges Simenon again, having always been a fan of his work. Then, along came *Dandelion Dead*. It landed on my doormat, I read it and, despite the title, which I have never really been fond of, I loved it. Michael Chaplin's script was wonderfully written, and was exactly what I was looking for, so I agreed to do it."

With a budget of £2.5 million, Hodges had the task of filming four hours of television drama for London Weekend Television.

Set in the Herefordshire town of Hay-on-Wye in the 1920s, *Dandelion Dead* is based on a true story. In January 1922, the arrest of local solicitor Major Herbert Armstrong was the talk of the town. He is a man at war on three fronts: his domineering wife, his pushy business rival and the dandelions that have colonized his front lawn. He learns that arsenic will solve the dandelion problem. Will it take care of the others?

Michael Kitchen stars as Armstrong and Sarah Miles plays his bullying wife Katharine. She is back-tingling in her calculating humiliation. "A formidable woman Mrs Armstrong," comments a friend. Quite right. From her first piercing "Herbert", it is clear this is partly a study of household horror. Husband and wife loathe each other behind the veneer of a happy Edwardian couple. Kitchen is brilliant as a man boxed in by convention, always polite and rarely revealing his hatred of his wife. By the conclusion of the first two-hour episode, Katharine's nagging days are over. After a slow deterioration of her health, it seems Armstrong's marital strife is over too. Katharine is dead and it appears that Herbert poisoned her with arsenic bought to kill the dandelions.

That still leaves the problem of the young rival solicitor, Oswald Martin (David Thewlis). Martin is rapidly taking business from him.

When Martin receives an enormous box of chocolates through the post, his sister-in-law eats some and becomes ill overnight. Shortly afterwards, Martin is invited to tea with Armstrong and is handed a buttered scone with the now immortal words "Excuse fingers". Hours later, Martin is also violently ill.

Previous page: *Michael Kitchen as Major Herbert Armstrong in Hodges' TV drama* Dandelion Dead *(1992)*

Puzzled, the young solicitor calls in the help of his father-in-law, a local chemist, John Davies. They decide an analysis should be made of Martin's urine. They also send the chocolates to be analyzed at the same time. Lethal doses of arsenic are found in both.

Armstrong is arrested, and Katharine's body exhumed. When arsenic is found in her too, he is charged and hanged for her murder.

Diana Quick appears as Marion Glassford-Gale, the Major's possible motive for murder. Bernard Hepton is the local chemist, John Davies. Don Henderson is Chief Inspector Crutchett who has the awkward task of investigating one of Hay's leading residents.

Did Armstrong really poison his wife with arsenic and try to murder a rival solicitor in the same way? There was strong circumstantial evidence against Armstrong but no proof.

Filming in the Wye valley in Breconshire was an eerie experience for the stars. "Walking past the unmarked spot where Katharine Armstrong is actually buried was peculiar," says Kitchen.

The slight ambiguity in the story is deliberate, according to producer Patrick Harbinson. Although Armstrong was eventually convicted of murder and hanged, there remains a firm body of opinion in Hay, led by the solicitor who today lives in Armstrong's house, that he was framed. "It is true," says Harbinson, "that he would probably not have been convicted today."

There is certainly a view that Armstrong was hurriedly convicted on the orders of the Director of Public Prosecutions, who had been embarrassed by the outcry at the acquittal one year earlier of another solicitor, Harold Greenwood, from up the road in Llanelli. Greenwood was charged with poisoning his wife, with weed killer in the claret, for money and a mistress. But, unlike Armstrong, Greenwood had as defence counsel Marshall Hall, a George Carman of his day.

Martin Beales, a solicitor who now sits in Armstrong's chair in his old office and lives in Mayfield, Armstrong's house, suggested a more controversial version to LWT. The Armstrong family allowed him to study the original court documents from which he concluded that John Davies, the chemist who supplied the arsenic to Armstrong, and the father-in-law of Martin, was the villain of the piece. He thinks Katharine "who combusted at 48 and went completely potty" probably took the arsenic herself by accident. "The Martin evidence should not have been admitted," he says. "In 1920, the idea of Armstrong sending another man chocolates is incredible. There should have been an appeal."

Armstrong's daughter Margaret wanted the dramatization stopped. She and her late sister and brother had stopped a dramatized sermon by Edgar Lustgarten being shown on the BBC, but failed with *Dandelion Dead*.

Why did Michael Chaplin reject the Beales version of events? The writer says: "I don't actually reject that theory. I did think about it, but drama deals with events. There's not much room for ambiguity. If I'd taken the other route, I'd have to show that Katharine committed suicide and that Davies and Martin mounted some kind of ghastly conspiracy to get rid of Armstrong. I found that implausible. On the other hand, it's certainly true that Armstrong would not have been convicted today."

Hodges says he can't be completely sure about what actually happened way back then in 1922:

"People love conspiracy theories but the evidence did seem pretty irrefutable. Either way he was hanged, but who knows?"

This two-part dramatization of a real-life story has superb direction, a terrific score (by Barrington Pheloung of *Inspector Morse* fame) and fine acting, not only by Kitchen and Miles, but also by David Thewlis as the rival solicitor who hastens the decline of Armstrong's business, Diana Quick as Armstrong's ex-mistress, and Robert Stephens in a delicious cameo as an eccentric landowner.

Dandelion Dead also proved, at the time, that exquisite costume drama doesn't have to be the preserve of the BBC. Hodges' dramatization is still regularly repeated on satellite and cable channels to this day, although in a sense it seems wasted on television. Edited down, *Dandelion Dead* could be a gorgeous, glossy feature film.

"I hadn't done television since *Squaring the Circle* and things had changed a lot. Although I had this amazing script, had got the magnificent Michael Kitchen in the lead role and Sarah Miles as well, I noticed how our crew seemed to be full of kids!

"There was me, the 64-year-old director; Gerry Fisher, the

cameraman, who must have been near 70; and Voytek who was 70-ish too. Gordon Haymen, my favourite operator, and Vangie Harrison, my favourite wardrobe designer, are also getting on. And then there was the rest who were all so young I couldn't believe it. I think they thought they had a real old crocks team at the helm of this production!

"But it was very interesting. They couldn't keep up with us. I actually reduced the shooting schedule so I could have more time in Hay-on-Wye. This made the producers really nervous. But having survived in this business this length of time, you intuitively know what to do. They could soon see we were moving cleanly and smoothly through the piece.

"Back in the late sixties, when I made *Rumour* and *Suspect*, once the script was approved, that was it and I was left to get on with it, even with the casting. Nowadays, television executives are obsessed with getting name actors in even the small roles. It's like directing in Madame Tussauds. One thing hasn't changed though – TV directors still get no residuals for repeats or overseas sales. For them, television has become a sweatshop.

"Nevertheless, it was a joy to do. I had a lovely time though and fell in love with Hay-on-Wye."

A year later, Hodges was offered another two-part television drama to direct, this time for the BBC. "It was my one and only experience of working for them," he says.

Called *The Healer* (1994), it was scripted by G F Newman – who had written *Law and Order* in the 1970s – and was about a young doctor who has the power of healing and the trouble it leads to.

"I liked the script very much. It was a bit like *Black Rainbow* in the sense that it catered for my enjoyment of things inexplicable. While I simply don't believe in God, I can still believe in the totally inexplicable."

The story centres around Dr John Lassiter, a mysterious young doctor (Paul Rhys) who finds he has a gift to heal when he brings a young boy out of a coma. He is hailed as a miracle worker but when his gift is misunderstood and when he fails to cure *en masse* the sick who have flocked to see him, everyone turns against him. His colleagues see him as a threat to medicine and the media want to expose him as a

fraud. In all of the hype, the actual miracle he performs goes unnoticed.

At the outset, Hodges was concerned that the two-parter would end up looking like *Casualty* or *Emergency Ward 10*. So he says he gave it a different feel by not cutting constantly. "By breaking the traditional rhythms of medical shows, I tried to break from that genre."

The Healer was transmitted on BBC1 in September 1994.

"Although I did have a very nice cast, *The Healer* was an absolutely awful film to shoot. We filmed in Merthyr Tydfil in Wales, a very deprived area full of poverty and ignorance. It was very grim. You'd hear a screech of tyres, look out of the window and see a car roll over, four kids would get out and run off. It was pretty shocking. We were told about young kids, under 10, going into A&E asking for needles. And how others had broken into the mortuary and thrown the dead bodies around. Horrible stuff.

"It didn't help that I fell out with G F Newman on our first day of shooting. He interfered with my direction, in front of the crew. That is unforgivable. I immediately called my agent and had him communicate to the BBC that I wouldn't continue unless he was banned from the set.

"I hadn't been told that Newman was a producer as well as writer when I agreed to do it. That inevitably leads to trouble in the editing room – and it did.

Did he do it? Michael Kitchen stars as Major Armstrong in Hodges' retelling of the famous Hay-on-Wye true story

"The climax of the piece is the 'miracle' the doctor actually performs – but which goes unnoticed. I shot it all terribly simply because I knew that if I elaborated it wouldn't be believable. Just read about the miracles in the *New Testament*. All the descriptions are plain and simple. 'He picked up his bed and walked.' And that was my inspiration. The doctor picks this young paraplegic up – he has fallen from his wheelchair – and puts him back in the chair. He walks off and never even sees the paraplegic's twisted limbs just unravel, like a flower opening up in the morning. It was raining when I shot this scene. I had the camera pan off the young man on to a tree. It so happened that as it reached the tree the sun came out and a light wind made the leaves shimmer. It was quite magical.

"But Newman wasn't satisfied. He wanted to sentimentalize the miracle, he wanted Puccini playing all over it, he wanted the paraplegic, now with perfect shining teeth, to get up and perform a jeté in slow motion. It was completely wrong, mad, laughable.

"I had made the film on a very small budget. It seems the BBC had subsequently got a foreign sale and, to my astonishment, allowed this money to be spent so that Newman could go out and re-shoot this. Needless to say it was a complete waste of money, public money to boot. The version actually transmitted was mine – so it worked out in the end! Another storm in a teacup."

The next few years were quiet. Hodges adapted Nicholas Blincoe's novel *Acid Casuals* for the screen but says he lost faith in the producers and declined to be involved as director.

"The good thing about writing as well as directing is that you can get a feel about the people you're working for *before* you actually go out there with a crew. A writer having his work screwed up is painful enough, but nowhere near as painful as being screwed as a director. If you are on an unhappy film as a director, life is hell. So by writing the script, you have time to find out the true nature of those you'll be working for as a director. If you sense it's going to be hell, get out.

"The same thing happened on *The Lifeforce Experiment* in 1994. I had adapted the Daphne du Maurier short story *The Breakthrough* for a film to star Donald Sutherland. But because of all of the changes they wanted to make to my script I knew it would be hell to direct and I declined. The film was eventually made, still with Donald Sutherland, directed by Piers Haggard."

It wasn't just film scripts Hodges was writing. Around the same time, he had begun work on his second stage play, *Shooting Stars and Other Heavenly Pursuits*. As it transpired, it would be a few years before it got a theatre.

"Writing for the theatre allows you to write about things you would never get into any other form. *Shooting Stars* was, like my 1985 play *Soft Shoe Shuffle*, a black and bleak comedy. In both, I was able to voice what I could never get away with on film or television.

"*Shooting Stars* is about the film industry. What else could it be other than surreal, demented and, hopefully, funny? The action takes place outside a megastar's suite in a luxury hotel. In one scene the bellboy is talking to Welty, the producer's assistant: 'When I'm watching movies I become somebody else. That's why I'm crazy for them.'

She replies: 'So was I. Until I worked on them.'

'You used to go a lot?'

'Three, four times a week. And every time my heart would stop when the curtains parted and the projector burst into life; cutting through the darkness; filling my life with colour and music. Now, when the lights go down the darkness stays. And I see only greed, hear only hype, feel only a sense of loss.'

"That's not one of the funny bits.

"My play is also a fairytale; a dark one. It's based on my experiences in the film industry during the late seventies and eighties. Painful at the time; funny in retrospect. As Hitchcock once said to an over-exercised actor: 'It is only a film.' That said, my litany of failure, mostly at the hands of North Americans, is long. My play carries the traces of the greed, egotism, narcissism, psychosis, stupidity and genuine insanity that I witnessed during this period; although I can never really do them justice."

Happily, Hodges' next film escaped being added to the list of disasters …but only just.

Beating the Odds:
Croupier and I'll Sleep When I'm Dead

"Everything is not under control. We may think we
have control but life is just a gamble. Things can
change quickly and radically."
Mike Hodges

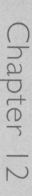

"Hodges' neonoir rivals Scorsese in his generous use of casino voice-over and weaves an unpretentious psychological thriller that stays gripping from the first frame. A fascinating study of human desperation." Stephen Garrett, film editor *Time Out New York*

Four years after completing his play *Shooting Stars and Other Heavenly Pursuits*, Hodges was asked by FilmFour, then under the stewardship of David Aukin, to make the film *Croupier* (1998). The story of an aspiring writer who takes a job as a croupier to make ends meet, it was written by Paul Mayersberg (who adapted *The Man Who Fell to Earth*). Hodges loved the script and instantly knew it had great potential. But the story of how *Croupier* made it to the big screen is almost worthy of a movie in itself.

Mayersberg and Aukin had been developing a story about a

"Hodges' neonoir rivals Scorsese in his generous use of casino voice-over and weaves an unpretentious psychological thriller that stays gripping from the first frame. A fascinating study of human desperation." Stephen Garrett, film editor *Time Out New York*

gambler for some time. Mayersberg explains:

"The origin of the film is a curious one. I had for many years tried to write a film about a gambler who plans a raid on a casino, but on the night of the robbery, he breaks the bank himself and so there is no money to steal. I could never quite make it work as the story was an anticlimax. I decided to look at it from another angle – to tell a story where fate intervenes to ruin the plans but good comes of it. If you gamble, you are aware of winning and losing streaks. I wanted to write a story where the two came together. In the original there was a character, who never spoke, he was just an observer – the croupier. I decided to tell his story. I switched everything around and the croupier became the hero, the minor character became central and the gambler disappeared.

Previous page: *Clive Owen as the intriguing protagonist Jack Manfred in Mike Hodges'* Croupier *(1998)*

"I was inspired by Kurosawa's samurai story *The Hidden Fortress*, in which the lead characters are hangers-on. In Japan, many attitudes are the complete reversal of the European. I took what I thought was a Japanese view of the story. I just kept the essence of the original ironic tale."

Jonathan Cavendish of Little Bird was approached to produce the film:

"The script immediately appealed to me. It is a very modern story with contemporary ideas, but told in a very classic manner. The first task was to find the right director. Both David and Paul had known Mike Hodges for years and I am a great fan of many of his films. The three of us all wanted to work with him, which was a happy coincidence. Mike is very good on atmosphere. The script was very intense and had a compelling quality which draws you into the story and Mike is able to do the same cinematically. I think all Mike's films have a theme: an individual within or against the system; but in this case, the individual realizes where he belongs."

Much of Mike Hodges' early documentary work for *World In Action* depended on observing life within organizations from oil companies to unions to political parties. "The story seemed relevant to the times we live in and had a complicated psychology. I was intrigued by the role of the croupier," says Hodges, explaining the project's appeal.

With Hodges on board, Cavendish put together a co-production between Channel Four, WDW/WDR and Tatfilm in Germany. Cavendish and Tatfilm had previously co-produced the BBC drama *The Writing on the Wall*.

Croupier was shot on location in and around London and at Info-Studios in Monheim, Germany. Clive Owen was cast as the central character, Jack Manfred. "Clive is extraordinary. He's the most precise actor I've worked with since Michael Caine. He also has an extensive knowledge of filmmaking and its rhythms," says Hodges.

Croupier is a remarkable film, one of the very best. Suspenseful, stylistically daring, wonderfully acted, it's as engrossing to watch as it is to listen to. A thriller for those with an adult's attention span – a deceptively simple tale with an unusually highbrow take on gambling.

Jack once worked in a casino in South Africa. Now living in England he is a struggling writer. His girlfriend Marion is keeping him by working as an undercover security guard in a department store. When his reprobate father calls from South Africa with a job offer in a London casino, Jack bites the bullet. Soon he's dealing blackjack and spinning the roulette wheel. "Welcome back, Jack, to the House of Addiction."

But Jack isn't addicted to gambling, he's addicted to "watching people lose". What a setting for his novel! Slowly, Jack gets entangled in the lives of his fellow workers and the casino's clientele.

What an entrance!
The glamorous
Jani De Villiers
(Alex Kingston)

Marion: I'm betting on you. Jack: I'm not much of a bet. Marion: You are to me.

But that was before Jack became a croupier. Working all night and sleeping all day, Jack's relationship deteriorates: "I want to live with a writer not a croupier. I don't even know what the word means."

Enter Jani. And what an entrance! She could be Lizabeth Scott in a B-movie as she sashays down the mirrored staircase of the casino. Jani is South African and ostensibly a rich gambler. Jack is intrigued. When they accidentally meet he starts to see her outside of working hours – a serious violation of casino rules. Jani's luck changes; she starts to lose and is soon being seriously threatened by loan sharks. Desperate, she approaches Jack, asking him to be the inside man for

"I liked the emotional world underneath the surface of the script, which is not immediately apparent. It's very economically written with quite a simple storyline, the casino is an analogy for something bigger." Mike Hodges

a planned heist at the casino. The sharks will pay him £10,000. Jack carefully considers the odds; at first he refuses. Then the novelist takes over and he goes for it.

Marion accidentally finds the cash advance that Jack has hidden, and then overhears a phone message from Jani. On the night of the robbery, police appear at the casino. Someone has grassed. The heist fails. While Jack is in the clear with the police, Marion gives him an ultimatum: quit the job or she'll tell the police about his involvement in the heist.

Jack returns to his book. One night the police come to his flat. Marion has been killed, apparently knocked down by a passing car. Jack wonders if it was really an accident and, full of guilt, finishes his novel.

The book *I Croupier* is published anonymously and instantly becomes a bestseller. Jack is rich. But there remains one last turn of the wheel. A phone call from Jani, now back in South Africa, reveals that she is about to get married to Jack's father. Jack had been set up from the beginning. As Jack puts it: "His father, 8,000 miles and 27 years away, was still dealing to his son Jack from the bottom of the deck …"

The last image brings the film full circle. The last scene is also the first, with the ball bouncing around the spinning roulette wheel. We see the frozen expressions of the punters. Then we hear Jack's voice: "Now he had reached the point where he no longer heard the sound of the ball … the spin of the wheel had brought him home to the place where he was born." With the hint of a smile as the ball falls into green zero: "The croupier's mission was accomplished. At last he was the Master of the Game. He had acquired the power … to make you lose."

With that, Jack rakes the chips off the table and into the black hole. The camera follows them into the blackness. Although this image wasn't in the shooting script, Hodges says it was imperative to the film:

"When I'd last gone to a casino the croupiers would collect and stack the chips by hand. Now I was astonished to find that they sweep them into this hole in the table, and into a machine below that stacks them. They do this right in front of the punters. The punters can literally see their bets going down the toilet. Nobody seems to notice or care. And yet each of those chips represents time, part of the punters' lives. And what had they had to do to earn the money to pay for the chips? When I saw that black hole I knew I had the end of the film."

Paul Mayersberg's screenplay is very cleverly structured. It was the script, says Owen, that attracted him to the project:

"I liked the emotional world underneath the surface of the script, which is not immediately apparent. It's very economically written with quite a simple storyline, the casino is an analogy for something bigger. The voice-over *is* the film for me. Without that it would be too elusive. Jack has a conversation with the audience throughout. Part of my decision was also Mike's involvement; he's a joy to work with, he's very experienced which is very important when you're making such a complex film.

"Jack is very cynical, very calculating," says Owen. "He doesn't play to whims and follies. He's elusive and doesn't give much away.

He goes on a journey to do this with his sense of security."

In the film Jack has relationships with three different women: Marion (Gina McKee), his girlfriend with whom he lives. He half-loves her but she wants it all. She is a romantic. He is her prisoner. Bella (Kate Hardie), a fellow croupier, shares his view of the life and demands nothing from him. Then there's Jani (*ER*'s Alex Kingston). Although she intrigues him he is suspicious of her. He isn't surprised to find she wants something from him.

When Marion asks Jack "What do I mean to you?" he replies, "You're my conscience." Marion reacts in shock: "Don't you have a conscience of your own?" Jack doesn't answer her.

Says Hodges: "We were lucky to get three very strong actresses. All three are very different. Gina delivers on the emotional level, puzzling all the time about the real Jack. Kate had the smallest role which, I think, is the most difficult because there's not a lot for her to get her teeth into – and yet she has to be memorable because she comes back in the last scene. And Alex is glamorous and mysterious. Playing a very devious (or is she innocent?) role, she conveys her character's amoral take on life beautifully."

All the actors were attracted by the elusive quality of the script. "The ambiguity and the enigmatic quality tempted me," explains Gina McKee. "I wanted to try to unravel it. It's a film about how you can fall in love with what you think someone is and when you find out that they're not as you thought, you try and control them."

Kate Hardie, who plays Bella says: "I liked the voyeurism of the script. I enjoy stories that are told from one character's point of view. The psychology of relationships and the way we gamble in relationships is a complex subject. When you write about people as Jack does, you start judging them; the narrator of the film is always telling you what he thinks of them. It's not clear whether he's a hero or not; it's quite ambiguous."

Hodges explains how he sees Jack's different relationships:

"While Marion loves Jack it's more his image rather than him. She's a romantic and living with a writer is part of that romantic illusion. Image is important to people, especially now. It comes from novels, films, television, glossy magazines. We're all liable to fall foul of it. *Croupier* is an uncomfortably truthful film about their relationship. I suspect it mirrors many real ones.

"Jani is a con woman and enjoys the role playing. She has to play it for real, just like an actress. She's completely amoral and never stops to contemplate the effect her deception will have on Jack. Confidence tricksters get absorbed by the game. They are programmed to succeed as much as anybody else, and have to meticulously go through the motions of pulling off the trick. The rush of adrenalin must be amazing.

"Bella demands nothing from Jack. She's really the only honest one, direct. It's not surprising they end up together, even more understandable given the father he's got."

Clive Owen's intense, minimal performance as Jack Manfred is the best of his career so far and his own third person voice-over gives the film an icy, distant quality. "That's the personality of the film," he points out. "Unusually, it wasn't narrative voice-over; it wasn't just filling in gaps in the narrative, it was like having a chat to the audience."

It's a huge credit to Owen that he makes such an internal role so absorbing to watch, but Hodges' depiction of the venal life of the casino is just as fascinating. "The reason it's such a strange, intense world is cash," states Owen. "We live in a world where everything is credit cards and everything is double checked. In casinos, you've got huge amounts of actual money changing hands all the time. Plus you get the whole spectrum of people. You get people gambling their last fiver and, in the same casino, millionaires putting thousands of pounds on blackjack."

Paul Mayersberg researched the subject by talking to croupiers about the ritual and procedure in casinos:

"A lot of the detail of the film has been supervised by experts in different departments. The psychology came from talking to croupiers. The most important aspect seemed to be how tedious the job is. The people who do it are attracted initially by the possibility of promotion and travel, but the price you pay is to be psychologically undermined. It's just like boarding school with its hierarchy, prefects and rules.

"I am resolutely not a gambler," continues Mayersberg. "It's seductive and undermines your life. I was interested to look at gambling from the point of view of a man who can't lose. He has contempt for gamblers and his kick is watching them lose. As a croupier, Jack's not typical because he refuses to gamble. His gamble is the writing connection. Writers all believe that, against the odds, they are going to be published and successful."

The casino was constructed over three weeks, in Germany's Monheim studio, by production designer Jon Bunker, based on one of the smaller London casinos. "Casinos have no windows or clocks and oxygen is pumped into the air so it's easy to lose track of time."

Hodges became fascinated by the concept of using mirrors. The idea came to him travelling on a bus, passing the HMV store in Oxford Street. "I remembered it had a wonderful staircase lined with mirrors," he recalls. "That was it. Mirrors I thought to myself. They

Is Jack more interested in calculating the odds on a card game than saving his relationship with Marion (Gina McKee)?

would give it lots of atmosphere – and enhance the sense of illusion, of things not being what they seem. Of course, they drove the camera crew crazy, keeping themselves and the lights out of every shot was not easy."

Jon Bunker adds: "Mike wanted to convey that sense of purgatory. The walls of mirrors gave a sense of the casino extending forever. It also has the effect that when Jack enters the casino, the reflection in the mirror conveys the idea of him walking away from himself."

Casino adviser David Hamilton was trained in Australia, on the Gold Coast in Queensland. He subsequently worked in casinos on cruise ships, in America, London and Russia, where he managed casinos and trained staff. In the film he plays a pit boss who runs several tables and as such, is responsible for the dealers. He also observes the customers, keeping a discreet eye on who's winning and sizing up their betting styles.

Clive Owen, Kate Hardie and Paul Reynolds were all trained in a casino school for four weeks by Carol Davis. "They were all very quick to pick it up, because as actors they are used to mimicry. They were very convincing," says Hamilton.

Owen had gambled in his time but "not in a casino". In his research, he learnt that "the house always wins and, because of that, deep down the croupiers know that the average punter is a mug".

Paul Mayersberg explains why the film is relevant to all of us: "The world of the casino is divided into gamblers and croupiers. The gamblers take risks and the croupiers have no risk at all; the odds are always in favour of the casino. We have a choice in life between working in the casino or the risk-taking of being a gambler. The question arises: do you want a life of security or a life of risk? The answer is: we want both."

Hodges was instantly attracted to the subject matter because of its relevance to contemporary life:

"Money is such a pivotal part of our lives now. It's always been essential, but this need has to be kept in perspective. There are other elements to one's existence that are more important than money. The idea of the casino and the croupier and the whole business of gambling seemed such an appropriate film to make.

"The film is also about writing. When I first read the script I just didn't believe the character was a writer. Paul and I had to work hard for about six months to try to make Jack believable as a writer. Not a great writer, probably a bad one, but he had to have that drive and urgency to complete a novel. In the end he writes only one – and knows that's it. It's partly about the romantic image of a writer. I had Mickey King say in *Pulp*, 'being a writer is great, it's the writing that's the problem'. That still stands. Of course it's partly Marion driving Jack. For instance, when he's writing he wears a fedora, a B-movie image of the writer. We don't know where this ridiculous ritual comes from until, in one scene, Marion finds him at work and isn't wearing his hat. She places it on his head and he carries on banging away at the word processor. Not a word is said."

Croupier crosses emotional and psychological boundaries in a most unusual way. Perhaps because it so closely parallels the experience of our own dreaming states, it gives us the opportunity – if not the illusion – of living in someone else's skin, and of rehearsing our own future.

Interestingly, when the film was released, comments on internet movie message boards seemed to focus on Marion's death. Many seemed confused, thinking Marion was killed for her part in preventing the robbery. Of course, those who "got it" realized that her death really *was* an accident. The film is all about chance. It shows how our lives are so contingent and hang on such absurd threads – where seemingly meaningless everyday decisions can lead anywhere, even to death.

Hodges claims the preoccupation with death in most of his films stems back to his Catholic upbringing: "Irrespective of the fact that I shed Catholicism decades ago, I am always conscious of death because it was embedded in me at a formative age. No bad thing either. Mortality is the great leveller."

For Hodges, the most underestimated element in filmmaking is the use of sound. In *Croupier* even more than most:

"The sound of the ball spinning on the wheel is the most important sound in the film. Taking the casino itself as a metaphor, we spread that sound outside of that space and into Jack's other life. After all it isn't just in casinos that chance rules. It's everywhere.

"The FilmFour executives could never really understand that concept and when I finally showed them the film, they asked me why I didn't do what I said I'd do. They must either be deaf or too afraid to stop and listen. Busy people often stop listening. The sound of the ball and wheel spinning is the first thing you hear. And the last."

When Hodges delivered the finished film back in 1999, the reaction from FilmFour was not encouraging. The film was about to be abandoned. David Aukin, who commissioned the original script, had taken a dislike to it, claiming the only thing he liked about it was the "end credits". So *Croupier* languished without a distributor until the British Film Institute, re-releasing *Get Carter* at the time, picked it up and screened it in its small network of cinemas.

"As the BFI were reissuing *Get Carter*, my first cinema film, I suggested they may like to release my latest film. They agreed and undoubtedly saved it from going straight to video. Despite being critically well received, the two prints limped around the country, hardly seen by anybody. The BFI simply didn't have the resources to capitalize on the reviews, and FilmFour was not prepared to help. Then something bizarre happened. And not in the UK.

"The film's fate started to improve – and in the unlikeliest of places. I'd sent a video of it to an old friend in Los Angeles. Mike Kaplan has marketed films for Stanley Kubrick, Lindsay Anderson and Robert Altman, among others, and he's brilliant at it. He is also a rare creature in this infernal industry; being honest, passionate, and loyal to the point of obstinacy. Mike loved *Croupier*, and set about getting a US distributor. It took him over a year before he got a deal – but he got it!. During that time he wasn't being paid, and had to constantly keep FilmFour at bay. They were anxious to complete an impending television sale."

Croupier opened in the US on 21 April 2000 with just 17 screens guaranteed for two weeks. In sometimes dodgy venues and with very little advertising and marketing money being spent on it, the reviews were amazing. So good, they simply couldn't be ignored. Through word of mouth, *Croupier* began to take off. "In some ways it was an unlikely contender for Main Street, America," says Hodges, "being a quiet, complex piece, problematic for those addicted to popcorn, with very little music, and a lot of voice-over, usually considered the kiss-of-death by the *cognoscenti*. In short, it's the antithesis of everything taught at those slick weekend courses on writing successful screenplays. It's not a script-by-numbers; it's a script about numbers."

"Hang on tightly; let go lightly," says Jack Manfred, the croupier. He echoed Hodges' feelings exactly.

"When I first heard that FilmFour was not interested in the film, I privately decided to let go lightly and jack in filmmaking altogether," he says. "Now, suddenly, a metamorphosis occurred. I was hot again. Every day a slew of script offers dropped through my letterbox. As the film burgeoned into cinemas across America, my peace was about to be disturbed. The phone never stopped ringing. People I hadn't heard from in decades made contact. Producers, writers, designers, actors, first, second and third assistant directors, forgotten friends. Among them Sam J Jones, who played the lead in *Flash Gordon*. We hadn't spoken since we finished the shoot in 1980. Even a landlady who'd rented me her Los Angeles apartment some 20 years earlier sought me out. My office floor was awash with fax paper spewing out reviews and *Variety* box office returns. The film eventually reached 150 screens. Each week it climbed further up the grosses chart. Two million dollars. Three. Four. Peanuts compared to *Gladiator* and *Titanic* but great for a film that cost only four, and with no TV or radio spots to help it in the market place."

Croupier became the biggest independent film that summer. With an endless stream of fantastic reviews, the film gathered momentum and ended up on 134 screens. It was celebrated in no less than 43 Ten Best Lists including those in *Rolling Stone Magazine*, the *LA Times*, *The Washington Post*, *Time Out New York* and *Film Comment*. Hodges was described as an "under-appreciated master of the medium" by the *New York Observer*, while *Newsday* enthused: "Mayersberg's words follow you home in the dark." Clive Owen's charismatic performance was compared to a host of stars, from Humphrey Bogart and Robert Mitchum to Sean Connery and Michael Caine.

Such was the impact of the film on American critics that they were soon talking up its Oscar chances. In particular, Owen was being singled out as a likely bet for a best actor nomination. Then the Academy of Motion Pictures ruled that *Croupier* was ineligible for the Oscars because it had been briefly released in Singapore the year before, as well as having been screened on Dutch television. Hodges was saved the embarrassment, and the cost of renting a tuxedo. "I'm no fan of that event," he smiles.

Owen also didn't seem that bothered about having missed out at the Oscars: "When I first heard the Oscar rumours, I thought, 'Oh yeah'. But then they started cropping up everywhere, and it was so well reviewed that you start to think: 'Well, you never know.' But, to be truthful, it's such a fantastic story for a little film to have a life like that. Ultimately, it's all about the work."

Then something even more satisfying occurred. Paul Webster, who had replaced David Aukin at FilmFour, called to tell Hodges they'd had second thoughts. Following the film's successful run in the US, they would distribute *Croupier* in the New Year. He kept his promise and the film re-opened in the UK on 1 June 2001.

To add to this delight, a friend of Hodges' youngest son rang him out of the blue. Lawrence Elman, actor and entrepreneur, had read his four-year-old play *Shooting Stars and Other Heavenly Pursuits*. He gave it to Ken McClymont, who runs the Old Red Lion, a 60-seater pub theatre in London's Islington and soon Hodges was directing the play. "There was no budget, which is novel," he explains. "The actors performed for no salary. FilmFour generously took an advert in the programme which paid for the rehearsal rooms and it opened to coincide with the re-release of *Croupier*."

Suddenly a hot property again, following the resurrection of *Croupier*, Hodges decided he could afford to sit back and take time to work out his next move. He was receiving numerous offers to direct a variety of different films, but in the end he put all of his efforts into a project he'd been trying to make for some time.

I'll Sleep When I'm Dead (2002), the story of a man forced into extreme violence by the male rape of his younger brother, had been on Hodges' agenda for nearly a decade:

"Nine years ago, a friend of mine, Trevor Preston, wrote a script called *I'll Sleep When I'm Dead* and asked me to read it. I loved it, but we had great difficulty in finding the right actor to play the lead.

"Later, while I was doing *Croupier*, I found that I really got on with Clive Owen and asked him to read Trevor's screenplay. Although Clive loved it, at that time it looked like *Croupier* was going down the toilet. No one was interested in distributing it in the UK, and needless to say, we couldn't find the finance. Admittedly, the screenplay was very dark, which didn't help.

"*Croupier* then became immensely successful in America, was redistributed in the UK and then, of course, people started taking interest in what else I had to offer – which was *I'll Sleep When I'm Dead*. Now people were interested. It just shows how completely asinine the movie business is. The script hadn't changed; Clive Owen hadn't changed, I hadn't changed. What had changed was people's perception of us!

"It did feel very odd when the project suddenly came together in the way it did. Remember that *Croupier* wasn't released properly until 2001, and while people assume it is a recent film, I'd filmed it back in 1998. When *I'll Sleep When I'm Dead* eventually came together, I started worrying. Was it as good as I remember? I was even scared to read the script again. I hadn't looked at it for over a year. As it was four years since I'd made a film, had my directing skills evaporated? But, as always happens when I'm about to make a film, I turned into a sponge, absorbing everything around me. I like to be open to every sound and every image, which can often take on a new resonance, accidental offerings, anything that might add some little touch to the film.

"Of course, any nervousness stems from the fear that inspiration won't arrive in time. Or that the film won't reveal itself to you. So it's important to stay relaxed through this period. If you're too uptight you'll fail to notice these moments. It's a bit like being a jazz musician in that you have to relax, let the music come through you, hoping that any improvization pays off and everything comes together. The best films have a sense of being improvized with the director letting the film itself tell you what it wants. Sounds mad but letting the film do that is really important. Each one has its own identity."

I'll Sleep When I'm Dead was offered to FilmFour but Paul Weston admitted that he found it too bleak, and turned it down. He did, however, commission a script from Paul Mayersberg based on a synopsis by Hodges. Its working title is *Stripped*.

Mike Kaplan, who masterminded *Croupier*'s US success, is producing *I'll Sleep When I'm Dead*. With Paramount Classics guaranteeing American distribution he approached the independent film company Revere Pictures and obtained a budget of $6.5 million. As well as Clive Owen and Jonathan Rhys-Myers, the film also features Malcolm McDowell and Charlotte Rampling.

"The film is about a criminal boss, Will Graham, trying to escape from the milieu of violence and depravation he was born into. Just like Jack Carter. But unlike Carter, he's become a recluse. A bum constantly on the move. Our story reveals how he is relentlessly sucked back into his old life, a place that his younger brother still inhabits.

"My opinion of the project changed drastically when I returned to it after all these years. Because I see the world as such a dangerous place right now, maybe more so than ever before, and because revenge is much on our minds, our film has an added urgency .

"It also touches on a curious homo-erotic zone that now seems to be more apparent. I've noticed that in a lot of 'buddy' films, particularly war films, the male bonding has an undercurrent of sexuality. It's the exclusion of women that creates a sexual vacuum in which many men seem happy. They seem to like it best when they are in a uniform. Interesting that homosexuality was so prevalent among the Nazis? I suppose sexually ambiguous men will deliberately seek out occupations or sports that bring them into exclusive contact with other men. Undoubtedly most of us, especially 'jocks', are scared to examine their sexuality. In *I'll Sleep When I'm Dead* these genies are unleashed, revenge and horror, but horror of sexual humiliation in a macho world. Every night, on the television news, I watch this macho world going about its business, and Trevor's script takes on more relevance even than when I first read it.

"In a way it is a samurai film. Once a samurai always a samurai. As with Jack Carter, Will can't escape his past. None of us can, of course. On a broader canvas it's about man trying to climb out of the slime but always seeming to slip back into it. It's a pretty depressing thought, but then I have a very black view of humanity overall. I rest my case every single day – with the News. So, our film is a tragedy."

One of the most exciting parts of making any film for Hodges is finding the locations, *I'll Sleep When I'm Dead* was no exception:

"Looking for locations is like searching for another character. I prefer to go on my own because the locations spark off ideas that you can only explore without interruption. This process is a very big part of putting the jigsaw together. The locations begin to affect everything, the script, the cast and obviously the way the film is going to look.

"The rape scene will be heavily influenced by the location I find, and allow me to do it with discretion but letting the horror and loneliness seep into the scene."

With *I'll Sleep When I'm Dead* Hodges has been drawn yet again to dark subject matter. His Catholic upbringing, the early experience of adult betrayal and the subsequent losing of his faith won't seem to let go of him. We all live in a world full of death but don't dwell on it. Hodges is constantly aware of his own death, always conscious of his

> "The most important thing is to get the film made the way you want it." Mike Hodges

own mortality. This may explain why many of his films are so bleak: reminders to us of our mortality. But it's definitely the living that nurtures his obsession with human exploitation, which he has seen a-plenty:

"Democracy is an illusion because the politicians are interchangeable. But then choice itself is an illusion when conformity is the reality. Everything is becoming the same. The people with real power, bureaucrats and corporate bosses, answer to no one. It's blatant. We're so powerless they don't even bother to hide rip-offs and corruption any longer.

"The irony is that if I wanted to discuss this, or in any way question capitalist values, I have chosen to do it in the most expensive of all mediums! And film financing itself wouldn't bear too close an

Hot again. Since the success of Croupier, *film industry folk are clamouring to Get Hodges...*

examination. On one film I made, virtually everybody involved in the financing ended up in trouble with the law! One went to jail and one absconded with a considerable sum of money and hasn't been seen since!

"I'm sad that socialism is so discredited. Of course, it wasn't socialism that let us down, it was the other way around. That's worth remembering. We embraced the law of the jungle instead – and we're paying for it. That's what my films are really about. Maybe we'll turn things around in time – but I doubt it."

It is precisely because Hodges chose to make uncompromising films that he's made so few. Apart from his television projects, he's made just nine films in 30 years. But this is how Hodges likes it. He is not driven by quantity. After a painful time in the 1980s, making movies to survive, he has discovered that, in the end, it is only the personal films that matter. Hodges cites *Pulp, Black Rainbow* and *Croupier* as his favourites. They were personal to him and, in the end, all found an audience.

"The most important thing is to get the film made the way *you* want it. Before the success of *Croupier*, I had reconciled myself to the fact that my films were not destined for proper distribution, and began to think of them as 'messages in bottles'. When the message is safely in the bottle, let go, don't even watch it float off. It will wash up somewhere. Just as *The Terminal Man* is finding an audience now; as *Black Rainbow* found a substantial audience in Japan, and as *Croupier* came back home to find an audience the second time around."

And so Mike Hodges is on the up. The success of *Croupier* has made him cool again. Retrospectives of his work have recently been staged at both the Museum of Modern Art in New York and the American Cinematheque in Los Angeles.

He is currently working on treatments of the Thomas Mann story *Mario and the Magician* and his own script *Grist*, and in the meantime he is in talks with MGM, which now owns the rights to *A Prayer for the Dying*. The studio has invited him to restore it to its original version.

"I'm a hot director again! Just like I was in the early seventies. It's as if I'd been discovered in a peat bog, dug up and dusted down. What a joke!"

Filmography

The following films are those which Mike Hodges wrote and/or directed.

Suspect (UK, 1969, 80m, TV film)
Production Company: Thames
Director: Mike Hodges
Producer: Mike Hodges
Executive Producer: Lloyd Shirley
Screenplay: Mike Hodges
Camera: Michael Rhodes
Sound: Basil Rootes
Film Editor: Mike Taylor
Dubbing Mixer: Mike Billings
Production Designer: Patrick Downing
Music: Norman Kay
Cast: Rachel Kempson (Phyllis Segal), Bryan Marshall (Mark Segal), George Sewell (DI Barnes), Michael Coles (DS Jagger), Jean Alexandrov (Jean Segal), Roger Rowland, Russell Hunter, Dorothy White, Christopher Banks

Rumour (UK, 1970, 80m, TV film)
Production Company: Thames
Director: Mike Hodges
Producer: Mike Hodges
Executive Producer: Lloyd Shirley
Screenplay: Mike Hodges
Camera: Dusty Miller
Script Editor: George Markstein
Sound: Basil Rootes
Film Editor: Peter Lee-Thompson
Production Designer: Patrick Downing
Music: Moody Blues
Cast: Michael Coles (Sam Hunter), Ronald Clarke (The Assassin), with Mary Baxter, Joyce Blair, Kevin Brennan, John Caeser, David Cargill, Martin Carroll

Get Carter (UK, 1971, 112m)
Production Company: MGM / Released by MGM-EMI
Distributors Ltd
Director: Mike Hodges
Producer: Michael Klinger
Screenplay: Mike Hodges
Photography: Wolfgang Suschitsky
Editor: John Trumper
Music: Roy Budd
Art Director: Roger King
Production Designer: Assheton Gorton
Cast: Michael Caine (Jack Carter), Ian Hendry (Eric Paice),
Britt Ekland (Anna Fletcher), John Osborne (Cyril Kinnear),
Tony Beckley (Peter), George Sewell (Con McCarty),
Geraldine Moffat (Glenda), Dorothy White (Margaret),
Rosemarie Dunham (Edna), Petra Markham (Doreen), Alun
Armstrong (Keith), Bryan Mosley (Cliff Brumby), Glynn
Edwards (Albert Swift), Bernhard Hepton (Thorpe), Terence
Rigby (Gerald Fletcher)

Pulp (UK, 1972, 95m)
Production Company: United Artists
Director: Mike Hodges
Producer: Michael Klinger
Screenplay: Mike Hodges
Photography: Ousama Rawi
Editor: John Glenn
Music: George Martin
Art Director: Darrell Lass
Production Designer: Patrick Downing
Cast: Michael Caine (Mickey King), Mickey Rooney (Preston
Gilbert), Lionel Stander (Ben Dinuccio), Lizabeth Scott (Princess
Betty Cippola), Nadia Cassini (Liz Adams), Dennis Price
(Mysterious Englishman), Al Lettieri (Miller), Leopoldo Trieste
(Marcovic), Amerigo Tot (Partisan), Robert Sacchi (Jim

Norman), Giulio Donnin (Typing Pool Manager), Joe Zammit Cordina (Santana), Luciano Pigozzi (Del Duce), Maria Quasimodo (Senora Pavone)

The Terminal Man (US, 1974, 103m)
Production Company: Warner Bros.
Director: Mike Hodges
Producer: Mike Hodges
Screenplay: Mike Hodges (based on Michael Crichton's novel)
Photography: Richard H Kline
Editor: Robert L Wolfe
Music: "Goldberg Variation No. 25" by J S Bach, performed by Glenn Gould
Art Director: Fred Harpman
Cast: George Segal (Harry Benson), Joan Hackett (Dr Janet Ross), Richard A Dysart (Dr John Ellis), Donald Moffat (Dr Arthur McPherson), Michael C Gwynne (Dr Robert Morris), William Hansen (Dr Ezra Manon), Jill Clayburgh (Angela Black), Norman Burton (Det. Capt. Anders), James Sikking (Ralph Friedman), Matt Clarke (Gerhard), Jim Antonio (Richards), Gene Borkan (Benson's Guard), Dee Carroll (Night Nurse)

Damien: Omen II (US, 1978, 109m)
(Hodges left as Director after three weeks' shooting. Replaced by Don Tayler. Hodges did, however, receive credit for the screenplay)
Production Company: Twentieth Century Fox
Director: Don Taylor
Producer: Harvey Bernhard, Charles Orme
Screenplay: Mike Hodges, Stanley Mann
Photography: Bill Butler
Editor: Robert Brown
Music: Jerry Goldsmith
Art Director: Philip M Jefferies
Cast: William Holden (Richard Thorn), Lee Grant (Ann Thorn),

Jonathan Scott-Taylor (Damien Thorn), Robert Foxworth (Paul Buher), Nicholas Pryor (Charles Warren), Lew Ayres (Bill Atherton), Silvia Sidney (Aunt Marion), Lance Henrikson (Sergeant Neff), Elizabeth Shepherd (Joan Hart), Lucas Donat (Mark Thorn), Allan Arbus (Pasarian)

Flash Gordon (UK, 1980, 110m)
Production Company: Universal/De Laurentiis
Director: Mike Hodges
Producer: Dino De Laurentiis
Screenplay: Lorenzo Semple Jr
Photography: Gil Taylor
Editor: Malcolm Cooke
Music: Howard Blake, Queen
Art Director: Danilo Donati
Cast: Sam J Jones (Flash Gordon), Melody Anderson (Dale Arden), Max von Sydow (The Emperor Ming), Topol (Doctor Hans Zarkov), Ornella Muti (Princess Aura), Timothy Dalton (Prince Barin), Brian Blessed (Prince Vultan), Peter Wyngarde (Klytus), Mariangela Melato (Kala), John Osborne (Arborian Priest), Richard O'Brien (Fico), John Hallam (Luro), Philip Stone (Zogi, the High Priest), Suzanne Danielle (Serving Girl), William Hootkins (Munson)

Missing Pieces (US, 1983, 96m)
Production Company: CBS
Director: Mike Hodges
Producer: Doug Chapin
Screenplay: Mike Hodges (based on Karl Alexander's novel)
Photography: Charles Correll
Editor: Jim Oliver
Art Director: Fred Harpman
Cast: Elizabeth Montgomery (Sara Scott), Ron Karabatsos (Claude Papazian), John Reilly (Sam), Louanne (Valerie Scott),

Robin Gammell (Senator Lawrence Conrad), Julius Harris (Spencer Harris), David Haskell (Andy), Daniel Pilon (Jorge Martinez), Virginia Paris (Anna Perez), Leslie Ackerman (Judith Rosenus), Martin Azarow (Hector Bolinas), David Byrd (Motel Manager), Burke Byrnes (2nd Man Hood), Daniel Currie (Doctor), Lou Cutell (Man)

And the Ship Sails On (France/Italy, 1983, 132m)
(Hodges dubbed the English version of this Fellini film)
Director: Mike Hodges
Producer: Franco Cristaldi
Screenplay: Catherine Breillat, Roberto De Leonardis (Italian dialogue adaptation), Federico Fellini, Tonini Guerra
Photography: Giuseppi
Editor: Ruggero Mastroianni
Art Director: Maria-Teresa Barbasso
Music: Gianfranco Plenizio
Cast: Freddie Jones (Orlando), Barbara Jefford (Ildebranda Cuffari), Victor Poletti (Aureliano Fuciletto), Peter Cellier (Sir Reginald J Dongby), Elisa Mainardi (Teresa Valegnani), Norma West (Lady Violet Dongby Albertini), Paolo Paoloni (Il Maestro Albertini), Sarah-Jane Varley (Dorotea), Fiorenzo Serra (Il Granduca), Pina Bausch (La Principessa Lherimia), Pasquale Zito (Il Conte di Bassano), Linda Polan (Ines Ruffo Saltini), Philip Locke (Il Primo Ministro), Jonathan Cecil (Ricotin), Maurice Barrier (Ziloev)

Squaring the Circle (UK/US, 1984, 120m)
Production Company: TVS/Metromedia Producers Corporation/Britannic Film and Television
Director: Mike Hodges
Producer: Frederick Brogger
Screenplay: Tom Stoppard
Photography: Michael Garfath

Editors: John Bloom, Eric Boyd-Perkins
Production Designer: Voytek
Cast: Richard Crenna (Narrator), Bernard Hill (Lech Walesa),
Alec McCowen (Rakowski), Roy Kinnear (Kania), John
Woodvine (Geirek), Richard Kane (Jaruzelski), Don Henderson
(Kuron), Frank Middlemass (Brezhnev), John Bluthal (Babiuch)

Morons from Outer Space (UK, 1985, 97m)
Production Company: Thorn EMI, distributed by Columbia-
EMI-Warner
Director: Mike Hodges
Producers: Barry Hanson, Verity Lambert
Screenplay: Griff Rhys Jones, Mel Smith, developed by Bob
Mercer
Photography: Phil Meheux
Editor: Peter Boyle
Music: Peter Brewis
Art Director: Terry Gough, Bert Davey
Production Designer: Brian Eatwell
Cast: Mel Smith (Bernard), Griff Rhys Jones (Graham Sweetley),
James Sikking (Colonel Laribee), Dinsdale Landen (Commander
Matteson), Jimmy Nail (Desmond Brock), Joanne Pearce (Sandra
Brock), Paul Bown (Julian Tope), Sean Barry-Weske (Doomsday
Man), Edward Arthur (Television Interviewer – UK), Tim Barker
(Mathematician), Joss Buckley (TV presenter), Richenda Carey
(Countess Gretel), John Clamp (Bobby), Susan Denaker (Nurse
1), Robin Driscoll (Space Pilot), Graham Fellows (Cipher)

Florida Straits (US, 1986, 97m)
Production Company: HBO Pictures/Robert Cooper Films
Director: Mike Hodges
Producer: Stuart B Rekant
Screenplay: Roderick Taylor
Photography: Dennis C Lewiston

Editor: Edward M Abroms
Music: Michel Colombier
Art Director: Mack Pittman
Production Designer: Voytek
Cast: Raul Julia (Carlos Jayne), Fred Ward (Lucky Boone), Daniel Jenkins (Mac), Jaime Sanchez (Innocente), Victor Argo (Pablo), Ilka Tanya Payan (Carmen), Antonio Fargas (El Gato Negro), Jesse Corti (Guido), Raul Davila (Esteban), Simon Frederick (Beer Handler), Ed Grady (Lenny), Olivia Griego (Carmen's Daughter), Mario R Griego (Patrol Boat Captain), Dani Gulledge (Danny's Girlfriend), Cedric Guthrie (Danny)

A Prayer for the Dying (US, 1987, 105m)
Production Company: HBO Pictures/Robert Cooper Films
Director: Mike Hodges
Producer: Peter Snell, Sam Goldwyn Jr
Screenplay: Edmund Ward (based on Jack Higgins's novel)
Photography: Mike Garfath
Editor: Peter Boyle
Music: Bill Conti
Art Director: Martyn Herbert
Production Designer: Evan Hercules
Cast: Mickey Rourke (Martin Fallon), Bob Hoskins (Father Da Costa), Alan Bates (Jack Meehan), Sammi Davis (Anna), Christopher Fulford (Billy), Liam Neeson (Liam Docherty), Leonard Termo (Bonati), Camille Coduri (Jenny), Maurice O'Connell (Miller), Alison Doody (Siobhan Donovan), Karl Johnson (Fitzgerald), Ian Bartholomew (Kristou), Peggy Aitchison (Mrs Orton), Cliff Burnett (Varley), Anthony Head (Rupert)

Black Rainbow (UK, 1990, 95m)
Production Company: Goldcrest
Director: Mike Hodges

Producers: John Quested, Geoffrey Helman
Screenplay: Mike Hodges
Photography: Gerry Fisher
Editor: Malcolm Cooke
Music: John Scott
Art Director: Patricia Klawonn
Production Designer: Voytek
Cast: Rosanna Arquette (Martha Travis), Jason Robards (Walter Travis), Tom Hulce (Gary Wallace), Mark Joy (Lloyd Harley), Ron Rosenthal (Irving Weinberg), John Bennes (Ted Silas), Linda Pierce (Mary Kuron), Olek Krupa (Tom Kuron), Marty Terry (Mrs Adams), Ed Grady (Geoff Mcbain), Jon Thompson (Jack Callow), Helen Baldwin (Eva Callow), Darla N Warner (Shirley Harley), Christopher L Gray (Choirmaster), Lucy Williams (Choirlady)

The Lifeforce Experiment aka The Breakthrough
(UK / Canada, 1994)
(Hodges was the screenwriter only.)
Production company: Filmline International Inc. / Screen Partners Ltd
Director: Piers Haggard
Producer: Nicholas Clermont
Screenplay: Mike Hodges, Gerard Macdonald (based on Daphne du Maurier's story *The Breakthrough*)
Photography: Peter Benison
Music: Osvaldo Montes
Editor: Yves Langlois
Production Designer: John Meighen
Cast: Donald Sutherland (Dr "MAC" MacLean), Mimi Kuzyk (Jessica Saunders), Vlasta Vrana (Dr Robbie Allman), Corin Nemec (Ken Ryan), Hayley Reynolds (Niki Janus), Miguel Fernandes (George Cornwall), Michael Rudder (Woddy Gifford), Michael J Reynolds (Jack Aspect), Bronwen Mantel (Gaylene Janus), Peter Colvey (Victor Janus), Richard Zeman (Shepherd),

Ann Page (Receptionist), Henderson Walcott (US Marine), Philip Pretten (Attache), Michael Caloz (Ken – 9 years old)

The Healer (UK, 1992, 2 x 60m episodes)
Production Company: BBC
Director: Mike Hodges
Producers: Clive Brill, G F Newman
Screenplay: G F Newman
Editor: John Richards
Cast: Teresa Banham (Ann Meadrow), Leo Brightmore (Thomas Price), Michael Britton (Simon Major), Robert Brydon (Sean), Julie Covington (Madeleine Harland), Julia Ford (Dr Martha Fairbrass), Helen Griffin (Sister Day), Nicky Henson (Dr Ralph Raebryte), Fraser James (Jack Dark), Richard Lynch (Dave Major), Hilary Mason (Mary Simpson), Celia Montague (Elaine Price), David Norman (Peter Spinks), Richard Rees (Dr Paul Wem), Paul Rhys (Dr John Lassiter), Melanie Walters (Gill Major)

Dandelion Dead (UK, 1993, 4 x 60m episodes)
Production Company: London Weekend Television
Director: Mike Hodges
Producers: Patrick Harbinson
Executive Producer: Sarah Wilson
Screenplay: Michael Chaplin
Photography: Gerry Fisher
Editor: Malcolm Cooke
Music: Barrington Pheloung
Production Designer: Voytek
Cast: Michael Kitchen (Major Herbert Armstrong), Sarah Miles (Catherine Armstrong), David Thewlis (Oswald Martin), Lesley Sharp (Constance "Connie" Martin, née Davies), Peter Vaughan (Dr Hinks), Diana Quick (Marion Glassford-Gale), Bernard Hepton (Mr Davies), Robert Stephens (Henry Vaughan), Don

Henderson (Chief Inspector Crutchett), Chloe Tucker (Eleanor Armstrong), Alexandra Milman (Margaret Armstrong), Joseph Steel (Pearson Armstrong), Lucy Jenkins (Inez), Roger Lloyd-Pack (Phillips), Patrick Godfrey (Griffiths)

Croupier (UK, 1998, 91m)
Production Company: Channel Four Films/Little Bird/Tatfilm
Director: Mike Hodges
Producer: Jonathan Cavendish
Screenplay: Paul Mayersberg
Photography: Mike Garfath
Editor: Les Healey
Music: Simon Fisher Turner
Production Designer: Jon Bunker
Cast: Clive Owen (Jack Manfred), Alex Kingston (Jani de Villiers), Gina McKee (Marion), Kate Hardie (Bella), Nicholas Ball (Jack's Father), Paul Reynolds (Matt), Nick Reding (Max), Kate Fenwick (Cloë), Ozzi Yue (Mr Tchai), Tom Mannion (Ross), James Clyde (Gordon), Emma Lewis (Fiona), Ciro de Chiara (Arabic Man), Barnaby Kay (Car Dealer), Sheila Whitfield (Manicurist), John Radcliffe (Barber)

I'll Sleep When I'm Dead (UK, 2002, 90m)
Production Company: Will & Co Productions Ltd
Director: Mike Hodges
Producer: Eliza Mellor
Screenplay: Trevor Preston
Photography: Mike Garfath
Editor: Peter Boyle
Music: Simon Fisher Turner
Production Designer: Jon Bunker
Cast: Clive Owen (Will), Charlotte Rampling (Helen), Malcolm McDowell (Boad), Jonathan Rhys Meyers (Davy)

ABOUT THE AUTHOR

After graduating from Goldsmiths' College, University of London, Steven Paul Davies joined Virgin Radio, becoming the youngest-ever news presenter on national radio in the UK.

He is the author of *Alex Cox: Film Anarchist*, *The Prisoner Handbook* and *A–Z Cult Films and Filmmakers* and the co-author of *Brat Pack: Confidential*. He is based in Hereford and London.

www.stevenpauldavies.com

INDEX